SINNERS IN THE HANDS OF A LOVING GOD

IS GOD TRULY AN ANGRY JUDGE?

GIL HECKEL

Copyright © 2022 by Gil Heckel
First Paperback Edition

All rights reserved. No part of this publication may be reproduced, distributed, or transmitted in any form or by any means, including photocopying, recording, or other electronic or mechanical methods, without the prior written permission of the publisher, except in the case of brief quotations embodied in critical reviews and certain other noncommercial uses permitted by copyright law.
For permission requests, write to the publisher, addressed "Attention: Permissions Coordinator," at the address below.

Some names, businesses, places, events, locales, incidents, and identifying details inside this book have been changed to protect the privacy of individuals.

Unless otherwise noted, Scripture is taken from the
King James Version of the Bible, public domain.

Other Bible verisons used:

The Passion Translation® (TPT). Copyright © 2017, 2018, 2020 by Passion & Fire Ministries, Inc. Used by permission. All rights reserved. ThePassionTranslation.com.

The Living Bible (TLB). Copyright © 1971 by Tyndale House Foundation. Used by permission of Tyndale House Publishers Inc., Carol Stream, Illinois 60188. All rights reserved.

The Message (MSG). Copyright © 1993, 2002, 2018 by Eugene H. Peterson.

Amplified Bible (AMP). Copyright © 2015 by The Lockman Foundation, La Habra, CA 90631. All rights reserved.

The Companion Bible. Public Domain.

Contemporary English Version (CEV). Copyright © 1995 by American Bible Society For more information about CEV, visit www.bibles.com and www.cev.bible.

Darby Translation (DARBY). Public domain.

Easy-to-Read Version (ERV). Copyright © 2006 by Bible League International.

Expanded Bible (EXB). The Expanded Bible. Copyright © 2011 by Thomas Nelson Inc. All rights reserved.

Douay-Rheims 1899 American Edition (DRA). Public domain.

The Holy Bible, International Children's Bible® (ICB). Copyright© 1986, 1988, 1999, 2015 by Thomas Nelson. Used by permission.

The Holy Bible, New Century Version® (NCV). Copyright © 2005 by Thomas Nelson, Inc.

New Life Version (NLV). Copyright © 1969, 2003 by Barbour Publishing, Inc.

Wycliffe Bible (WYC). 2001 by Terence P. Noble

Complete Jewish Bible (CJB). Copyright © 1998 by David H. Stern. All rights reserved.

The Voice (VOICE) The Voice Bible Copyright © 2012 Thomas Nelson, Inc. The Voice™ translation © 2012 Ecclesia Bible Society All rights reserved.

American Standard Version (ASV). Public Domain.

English Standard Version (ESV) The Holy Bible, English Standard Version. ESV® Text Edition: 2016. Copyright © 2001 by Crossway Bibles, a publishing ministry of Good News Publishers.

New American Standard Bible (NASB) New American Standard Bible®, Copyright © 1960, 1971, 1977, 1995, 2020 by The Lockman Foundation. All rights reserved.

New Testament for Everyone (NTE) Scripture quotations from The New Testament for Everyone are copyright © Nicholas Thomas Wright 2011.

World English Bible (WEB) by Public Domain. The name "World English Bible" is trademarked.

J.B. Phillips New Testament (PHILLIPS) The New Testament in Modern English by J.B Phillips copyright © 1960, 1972 J. B. Phillips. Administered by The Archbishops' Council of the Church of England. Used by Permission.

Christian Standard Bible (CSB) The Christian Standard Bible. Copyright © 2017 by Holman Bible Publishers. Used by permission. Christian Standard Bible®, and CSB® are federally registered trademarks of Holman Bible Publishers, all rights reserved.

Amplified Bible, Classic Edition (AMPC) Copyright © 1954, 1958, 1962, 1964, 1965, 1987 by The Lockman Foundation

Geneva Bible of 1587. Public Domain.

Coverdale Bible of 1535. Public Domain.

Tyndale Bible of 1526. Public Domain.

Published by Freiling Publishing,
a division of Freiling Agency, LLC.

P.O. Box 1264
Warrenton, VA 20188

www.FreilingPublishing.com

PB ISBN: 978-1-956267-57-0
e-Book ISBN: 978-1-956267-58-7

Contents

Acknowledements vii
Introduction ix
1 What Is Love? 1
2 Old Testament Implications 11
3 Judgment 25
4 Defining Wrath 35
5 God's Nature and Plan from the Beginning 47
6 Cain 57
7 The Judgments 65
8 Resurrection of the Unjust 81
9 God's Plan 95
10 Romans 10 and 11 109
11 Weeping and Gnashing of Teeth 125
12 Weeping and Gnashing Continued 139
13 Many Are Called but Few Chosen 149
14 The Day of Christ and the Day of the Lord 167
15 The Day of God 187
16 Conclusion 197

Acknowledgments

I WOULD LIKE to take a minute to acknowledge all those who contributed to my life in pursuing the subject matter of this book. First, I would like to thank Dr. Victor Paul Wierwille who taught me the practical keys to the Word's interpretation.

I am especially thankful to Lawrence Panarello, whose book "The True Justice of a Just God" was the original inspiration for this one. He challenged me to see God's love bigger than I could ever have imagined.

I owe a great debt of gratitude to Peter Deleo who called me every few months for years, asking me what I had done for my book lately. And for years my answer was always the same: "nothing". It was his simple statement that motivated me to start: "You can't edit a blank page".

Thanks to our Bible fellowship from Columbia MO, who went along for the journey as we dug deeper into the truths set forth in this book.

Thanks to Kathy Gipson Doerscher, who went through the original manuscript with me, chapter by chapter providing valuable commentary along the way.

Thanks to Pat Schreiner, who went over the original manuscript after it was "completed" and gave me insights and corrections.

And of course, I am ever thankful for my wonderful family. My two girls, Brianna and Abbi, for whom I am very grateful and for whom I have great love.

And, last but certainly not least, my precious wife and spiritual partner who has helped me live practically so many of the truths set forth in the book. Her love and support mean more to me than I could ever fully communicate. Thanks Susie.

Introduction

THERE SEEMS TO be a rising tide of believers in the Christian community today that are recognizing the significance of the love of God. In reality, this is nothing new. As a matter of fact, the message from the early church for the first four or five hundred years was that of a loving, kind, and forgiving heavenly Father. The apostle John, writer of the gospel and epistles by that name and the one who received the inspiration for the book of Revelation, is believed to be the only member of the Twelve who died of natural causes. His final words are said to have been: "Love one another."

So what happened? The Christian world continued to suffer the type of persecution recorded in the gospels and the book of Acts, and its leaders continued to be martyred, so concessions were sought in the hopes of garnering peace with those who opposed their message. Then somewhere around the year 500, the world entered into what is known as the Dark Ages, and it was during this time that a new concept of God was established. The message of the original church changed and became one of an angry God who would be a stern judge committing many to hell, where they would be tormented and punished with eternal separation from him.

Could there be a connection between the viewpoint of God and the darkness of those ages? This theology continued on into the New World of America, where Christians sought a country and a form of government that would provide the freedom for them to pursue God as they understood him. Yet even in that setting, the "hellfire and brimstone" theology continued. This is evidenced by one of the prominent sermons delivered during the early days of the Great Awakening by Jonathan Edwards called "Sinners in the Hands of an Angry God."

Is it possible to get back to the original message of the church fathers, even though there have been 1,500 years of doctrine to the contrary? Is it possible to reconcile the loving heavenly Father of the early church with the angry God of wrath of the Dark Ages?

Yes, a thousand times yes. As a matter of fact, only within the context of love do the truths regarding the future judgments come into clear view, the darkness shrouding them dissipate, and the message of a loving, kind, and forgiving God shine through once again.

> *For God **so loved** the world, that He gave His only begotten Son, that whosoever believeth in Him should not perish, but have everlasting life. For **God sent not His Son into the world to condemn***

Introduction

***the world**; but that the world through Him might be saved. (John 3:16–17)*

God is not fickle, and he does not change his mind. As a matter of fact, his Word teaches just the opposite in the closing book of the Old Testament:

For I am the LORD, I change not. (Malachi 3:6)

These were some of the last recorded words of God before the world entered into a period of over 400 years without any new revelation or prophet speaking for him. But then something radically changed, and God gave us his only begotten Son who would come to unveil him in a way never seen before:

No one has ever gazed upon the fullness of God's splendor except the uniquely beloved Son, who is cherished by the Father and held close to his heart. Now he has unfolded to us the full explanation of who God truly is! (John 1:18 The Passion Translation)

God did not change, but our understanding of who he is was supposed to. God's omniscient plan was to send his Son, who would always perform his will perfectly and in so doing provide us a three-dimensional living, breathing illustration of who he really is. Jesus proclaimed: "He that hath seen me hath seen the Father" (John 14:9). What did Jesus' life and ministry communicate regarding God's disposition, and what does it tell us about the way he will handle the events of the future?

The overall goal of this book is to set before the reader a framework of biblical truths. These truths will fit together in such a way that they present a beautiful tapestry of a God who indeed is love and seeks only to save and not condemn mankind. While many are willing to accept this truth at face value, there are the "what abouts" that may arise, scriptures that seem to contradict that perspective, which I will endeavor to address in the coming chapters.

Before I go any further, let me set this disclaimer: While I believe the overall content of this book to be scripturally sound, I do not mean to say that it is perfect and without error. My goal is to set before you a foundation and new perspective on the truth to consider. When I first heard this subject matter presented about fourteen years ago, I did not believe it could possibly be true. As I set out to disprove it, much to my surprise, something else happened: I saw not only that it might be true but that it might actually be the key to connecting all the seemingly contradictory and confusing records about the future.

Introduction

My hope for you is the same. As you read through this book, please keep a list of questions that arise and see if they are not answered by the end. If not, I would like to know. If additional insights come to you, I would be interested to know about them as well. I truly believe that an accurate understanding of how God will handle the events of the future will help the reader approach that "perfect love" wherein there is no fear, and wherein the ability to speak boldly for him resides.

> *And we have known and believed the love that God hath to us. God is love; and he that dwelleth in love dwelleth in God, and God in him.* **Herein is our love made perfect, that we may have boldness in the day of judgment**: *because as he is, so are we in this world. There is no fear in love; but perfect love casteth out fear: because fear hath torment. He that feareth is not made perfect in love. (1 John 4:16–18)*

1

What Is Love?

THERE ARE THREE nouns that God uses in the Bible to define himself: spirit, light, and love. These three are singularly significant and will be explored in the coming chapters. With regard to love, that characteristic of the Father is recorded twice. Guess whose epistle records it? You got it—another inspiration from John:

> *He that loveth not knoweth not God; for* **God is love***. (1 John 4:8)*

> *And we have known and believed the love that God hath to us.* **God is love***; and he that dwelleth in love dwelleth in God, and God in him. (1 John 4:16)*

Notice the wording both times. It would be one thing to say, "God loves," which would leave room for the possibility that he does not love at times. But when the Bible states that God IS love, it leaves no room for anything else. It is his nature; he cannot do otherwise.

Whenever I approach the subject of reconciling the love and wrath of God, one of the most common responses I hear is: "Maybe we just don't understand love." And while love is as infinitely diversified as God himself, he did set apart a whole chapter in his Word to define it for us, so that we could know its major characteristics. And if God is love, then it can be said that these are qualities of God as well.

How interesting that the first quality of love listed in 1 Corinthians 13 is "suffereth long." This phrase is translated from one word in the Greek and is used only ten times in the New Testament, usually translated as "patient" or a derivative thereof. The Greek word in the Stephens text is *makrothumeo,* and it is defined as follows: "To be long tempered, long minded, slow to anger, and patiently forbearing." While some will look at "slow to anger" and conclude that God does eventually get angry, a closer look at the uses in the Bible clearly communicate that the length of patience demonstrated each time is "as long as needed to get the job done."

> *Be **patient** therefore, brethren, unto the coming of the Lord. Behold, the husbandman waiteth for the precious fruit of the earth, and hath **long patience** for it, until he receive the early and latter rain. Be ye also **patient**; stablish your hearts: for the coming of the Lord draweth nigh. (James 5:7–8)*

God is perfectly patient, as he is with every other aspect and quality of his nature. Later in 1 Corinthians 13, the apostle Paul records of love:

*Doth not behave itself unseemly, seeketh not her own, **is not easily provoked.** (1 Corinthians 13:5)*

And again, we have our "out." The way it reads in the King James Version gives the impression that God is provoked, but just not easily. And we might think that putting up with the foibles of humanity for thousands of years should be enough to provoke that anger.

Mankind wants God to have anger in his nature, because that is generally how he handles opposition and rejection. To know that God has his limit as well seems to bring a sense of comfort. However, like anything else, whenever the truth of the Word is changed, we bring unintended consequences upon ourselves. A deeper look into that passage reveals that the word "easily" is not in any of the other critical Greek texts. The statement is absolute: "is not provoked."

There is a very delicate yet vital balance between the doctrinal side of truth and the practical. Many truths can be fully understood only as they are lived. That is absolutely the case when it comes to love:

> *That Christ may dwell in your hearts by faith; that ye, being rooted and grounded in love, May be able to comprehend with all saints what is the breadth, and length, and depth, and height; And to know the love of Christ, which passeth knowledge, that ye might be filled with all the fulness of God. (Ephesians 3:17–19)*

The Amplified Bible translation of these verses makes it even clearer:

> *So that Christ may dwell in your hearts through your faith. And may you,* **having been [deeply] rooted and [securely] grounded in love, be fully capable of comprehending with all the saints (God's people) the width and length and height and depth of His love [fully experiencing that amazing, endless love]; and [that you may come] to know [practically, through personal experience]** *the love of Christ which far surpasses [mere] knowledge [without experience], that you may be filled up [throughout your being] to all the fullness of God [so that you may have the richest experience of God's presence in your lives, completely filled and flooded with God Himself].*

What Is Love?

The concept of love is meant to be experienced. It cannot be fully grasped in an academic setting alone. The way to truly understand love is to live it. That is why in the last evening Jesus spent with his disciples, it was his message again and again:

> *A new commandment I give unto you, That ye love one another; as I have loved you, that ye also love one another. By this shall all men know that ye are my disciples, if ye have love one to another. (John 13:34-35)*

Jesus knew from experience that the only way for his disciples to fully comprehend love and the God who is love would be to discipline themselves to love. It would be the true litmus test for all men to know for certain that they were his true followers.

> *This is my commandment, That ye love one another, as I have loved you. These things I command you, that ye love one another. (John 15:12, 17)*

Is it any wonder why these were the last words of John? He got the message and passed it on. And it is interesting to me that, out of all of Jesus' followers, God chose to unveil the book of Revelation to him.

These are just a few samples of the things Jesus taught on the last night he would be with his disciples in his physical body. The section of scripture in the gospel of John dedicated to that night, chapters 13 through 18, encompassing nearly 25 percent of that gospel, is one of the most love-saturated sections in the entire Bible.

The goal of all education should be action. Knowledge alone is just the beginning of the journey. Wisdom gained through experience should be our focus. If mankind for the most part has not lived up to the direction of the Lord—to love one another AS HE LOVED US—then it stands to reason that our understanding of love would be affected. It is not only the case that knowledge is to be experienced; it is also within the fabric of our hearts to view it through our experience. Could it be, therefore, that we have read into the concept of love our shortfalls and have attributed them to God?

> *Wherefore, my beloved brethren, let every man be swift to hear, slow to speak, slow to wrath: For the **wrath of man** worketh not the righteousness of God. (James 1:19–20)*

1 Corinthians 13:13, the final verse in the chapter on love, sets a parameter that is vital in getting the accurate doctrine on any subject in the Word. Love must be the

priority. It is the key to the practical fulfillment of truth in our lives as well:

And now abideth faith, hope, charity, these three; but the greatest of these is charity.

The "greatest" refers to the "estimation of things" or the priority given them, according to Bullinger's Lexicon. Of these three pillars of Christian life, love should be given priority when we read the Word of God to get the proper and accurate understanding. Everything needs to be viewed through the framework of love. The same is true as we live it. We need to discipline ourselves to love as Jesus taught to see the other two pillars evidenced in our lives, as recorded in this chapter as well:

*Beareth all things, **believeth** all things, **hopeth** all things, endureth all things. (1 Corinthians 13:7)*

When we are rooted and grounded in love, we will be able to believe all things, and we will have a hope that will enable us to endure all things.

Could it be, therefore, that our viewpoint of God has been tainted by our general failure to love as God does and as Jesus commanded? Has the "wrath of man" been subsequently read into and projected upon God and influenced our perception of Him? Let's take one final look at the Bible's listing of the attributes of love to see if there is any room for the anger that tends to be man's response to opposition:

Love never gives up.
Love cares more for others than for self.
Love doesn't want what it doesn't have.
Love doesn't strut,
Doesn't have a swelled head,
Doesn't force itself on others,
Isn't always "me first,"
Doesn't fly off the handle,
Doesn't keep score of the sins of others,
Doesn't revel when others grovel,
Takes pleasure in the flowering of truth,
Puts up with anything,
Trusts God always,
Always looks for the best,
Never looks back,
But keeps going to the end.
Love never dies.
(1 Corinthians 13:4–8 The Message)

Love is very patient and kind, never jealous or envious, never boastful or proud, never haughty or selfish or rude. Love does not demand its own way. It is not irritable or touchy. It does not hold

What Is Love?

grudges and will hardly even notice when others do it wrong. It is never glad about injustice, but rejoices whenever truth wins out. If you love someone, you will be loyal to him no matter what the cost. You will always believe in him, always expect the best of him, and always stand your ground in defending him. All the special gifts and powers from God will someday come to an end, but love goes on forever. (1 Corinthians 13:4–8 The Living Bible)

How does the concept of an angry, wrathful God fit with his description of love?

2

Old Testament Implications

WHEN IT COMES to the subject of the "angry wrath of God," most of the scriptural references that are used to build the case come from the Old Testament. Therefore, as we address this subject, it is prudent that we examine that topic now. Most everyone who has spent time in God's Word recognizes that there are definite distinctions between the Old and New Testaments. Even the titles alone signify that something changed: God has a ***new covenant*** with mankind. There are so many differences between the two that an entire book would need to be dedicated to the subject to do it justice. However, for the purposes of our topic, we are going to address only one aspect.

The term "old testament" appears only once in the entire Bible in the King James Version. Let's take a look at it and see if the passage defines the term for us and/or sheds any additional light on the subject:

> *But their minds were blinded: for until this day remaineth the same vail untaken away in the*

> *reading of the old testament; which vail is done away in Christ. (2 Corinthians 3:14)*

This scripture refers to the children of Israel not being able to look directly at Moses' face after his visitation with God. It is set as a figurative illustration to communicate a greater understanding as well: their inability to fully comprehend the truth. It goes on to say that the same veiled understanding remains today when reading the Old Testament, and only through the Lord Jesus Christ can that veil be removed. A saying that has been used in this context bears repeating at this time: "The Old Testament is the New Testament concealed; the New Testament is the Old Testament revealed."

The record in 2 Corinthians continues in verses 15 through 18:

> *But even unto this day, when Moses is read, the **vail** is upon their heart. Nevertheless when it shall turn to the Lord, the **vail** shall be taken away. Now the Lord is that **Spirit**: and where the **Spirit** of the Lord is, there is liberty. But we all, with open face beholding as in a glass the glory of the Lord, are changed into the same image from glory to glory, even as by the **Spirit** of the Lord.*

Old Testament Implications

Without going into too much detail, it is plain to see two things: the Old Testament is veiled, and only through the Spirit of the Lord can the veil be removed. The next logical conclusion can be derived: the veiled understanding was a senses perspective of spiritual realities. That is generally agreed upon to be the truth.

In the Old Testament, some believers had the Spirit upon them with certain conditions, and those men and women had an inside track to the truth. In the New Testament, when someone makes Jesus Christ his Lord, he receives the Holy Spirit and thus has the same access to the realities of the spiritual world. Mankind is sitting in the middle of a spiritual battle, and the Old Testament believers for the most part were not keenly aware of it.

For we wrestle not against flesh and blood, but against principalities, against powers, against the rulers of the darkness of this world, against spiritual wickedness in high places. (Ephesians 6:12)

It would have been terrifying for the men and women of the Old Testament to know about a spiritual battle with God's archenemy before it had been won by our Lord Jesus Christ. So God chose not to not clue them in. Instead, he chose to communicate those verities to them as if he were behind it all, and that he was the only one to look to for victory over things they could not see, touch, taste, smell, or hear. The figure of speech employed to accomplish this is called the Hebrew idiom of permission.

In his book, *Figures of Speech Used in the Bible*, E W Bullinger explains the idiom of permission this way:

> *Active verbs were used by the Hebrews to express not the doing of the thing, but the permission of the thing which the agent is said to do.**

It is not saying that God gave permission for these things to happen, but that he allowed himself to be attributed with doing them. Many times the scriptural references used to support the theology of an angry God of wrath are from the Old Testament, which presents a veiled perspective of God in which he chose to accept responsibility for what Satan was doing. But then something happened: Jesus the Christ, the Messiah and Savior of the world, was born. He would unveil the kingdom of darkness, defeat the devil, and give mankind a spiritual understanding of the unseen realm, so that he could triumph over God's archenemy as well.

Through this transition, one in which a kind, loving, and forgiving heavenly Father would be revealed by his Son, God declared in the closing scriptures of the Old Testament:

Old Testament Implications

For I am the LORD, I change not. (Malachi 3:8)

God did not change from the Old Testament to the New. What changed was our understanding and perception of him. Jesus took the lid off the enemy kingdom because he knew he would defeat it. He would also wrestle away the authority that had been extorted from Adam and give it back to mankind. It was time for humanity to have instruction on spiritual warfare and begin to take part in it. So God no longer needed the blame to be laid at his feet for what the evil one was doing. Not only was the veil regarding the activity of the devil removed, but the veil regarding the true nature of God could also be lifted:

> *No one has ever gazed upon the fullness of God's splendor except the uniquely beloved Son, who is cherished by the Father and held close to his heart. Now he has unfolded to us the full explanation of who God truly is! (John 1:18 The Passion Translation)*

Jesus stated, "He that hath seen me hath seen the Father" (John 14:9). He was the "Word made flesh" (John 1:14) and so was a living, breathing illustration of the nature of God for all to see. When we look at the records of his life in the gospels, we do not see him hurting anyone, refusing to heal anyone, or condemning anyone to hell. Instead, he manifested all the qualities listed in 1 Corinthians 13 as he moved among and ministered to the people. His ministry was summed up in Luke 4:18-19:

The Spirit of the Lord is upon me, because he hath anointed me to preach the gospel to the poor; he hath sent me to heal the brokenhearted, to preach deliverance to the captives, and recovering of sight to the blind, to set at liberty them that are bruised, to preach the acceptable year of the Lord.

He then wrapped up the scroll from which he was reading, while all eyes in the synagogue were fastened on him. The question is, why? Surely he was a fantastic teacher with charisma and held his listeners with rapt attention. But why is it specifically recorded here as though it were out of the norm? What does the Bible want us to recognize about this event?

Most likely, they were all familiar with this section of scripture from Isaiah; it was one that held the hope of the future for Israel. Those who might have begun to realize what he was saying, that he was the redeemer promised throughout the Old Testament, were excited about what was to come. But he stopped reading right in the middle of the verse and did not finish it.

Old Testament Implications

> *To proclaim the acceptable year of the* Lord, **and the day of vengeance of our God;** *to comfort all that mourn. (Isaiah 61:2)*

They wanted to see the "day of vengeance of our God" played out. That was not the purpose of Jesus' first coming to mankind, but it will be fulfilled at some point in the future. And here is where many go off on the "wrathful God" tangent. They see the word "vengeance," and in their minds they see the angry God coming with hellfire and brimstone. Yet the very context of this record in Isaiah communicates something else entirely. Even the last part of the verse gives us a clue: "to comfort all that mourn." The record goes on to say in verse 3:

> *To appoint unto them that mourn in Zion, to give unto them beauty for ashes, the oil of joy for mourning, the garment of praise for the spirit of heaviness; that they might be called trees of righteousness, the planting of the* Lord, *that he might be glorified.*

The New Testament word "vengeance" is defined in Bullinger's Lexicon this way: "Execution of right and justice, maintenance of right."** It appears that the execution and maintenance of justice and right, at least in this particular case, is more about restoration to the party that was wronged than about punishment inflicted on the wrongdoer.

Let's look at another scripture in the context of vengeance, this time from the New Testament:

Dearly beloved, avenge not yourselves, but rather give place unto wrath: for it is written, Vengeance is mine; I will repay, saith the Lord. (Romans 12:19)

Now we see the concept of wrath in the context of vengeance, and the reader can easily flip back to the angry God scenario. We will discuss in detail the concept of wrath in an upcoming chapter, but sticking to the use of vengeance in this verse, we see the following:

- It belongs to God, and man is not to seek it on his own.
- It is again described in terms of his repaying.

The immediate context both before and after sheds further light:

Recompense to no man evil for evil. *Provide things honest in the sight of all men. (Romans 12:17)*

Old Testament Implications

I remember the childhood phrase "Recompense to no man evil for evil" being expressed as the following: "Two wrongs don't make a right." And if there is any confusion as to exactly what is meant, the next verse adds:

If it be possible, as much as lieth in you, live peaceably with all men. (Romans 12:18)

Here we have what appears to be a condition with the word "if" starting the verse: "*If* it be possible ... live peaceably with all men." So it gives us another out. "God, in this situation, I can't live peaceably with these certain men," so I have some wiggle room. However, the ability to carry out this command is linked to "as much as lieth in you." This epistle was written to "the called of Jesus Christ" (Romans 1:6) and those who are "called to be saints" (Romans 1:7). What lies in the called of Jesus Christ and the called saints? The Holy Spirit of God, which is referred to as Christ in you. Therein lies a lot of ability to live peaceably with all.

The word "if" in verse 18 has an interesting twist to it. In *The Companion Bible*, E.W. Bullinger notes regarding its usage here:

Followed by the indicative mood, the hypothesis is assumed as an actual fact, the condition being unfulfilled, but no doubt being thrown upon the supposition.***

In other words, the phrase could literally be translated as "Since it is possible," and then the clause "as much as lieth in you" fits even more clearly. Since we now have the Spirit and therefore the nature of God in us, it is possible to live peaceably with all men, and thus this is the command. This is the verse that immediately precedes our scripture on vengeance and not avenging ourselves.

The verse immediately following gives us "what to do" to those who have wronged us:

Therefore if thine enemy hunger, feed him; if he thirst, give him drink: for in so doing thou shalt heap coals of fire on his head. (Romans 12:19)

Some have misinterpreted "heap coals of fire on his head" in a vengeful way. There's a little "hellfire and brimstone" for those who are looking for it. The idea is that if we carry out the instruction in this verse, we can really "burn our enemy." But the action given within the verse itself is to feed the hungry and give drink to the thirsty, so that application does not flow. Since we have the ability to live peaceably with all men, knowing that two wrongs don't make a right and that God will pay back whatever was taken from us, we are expected to take the high ground and not avenge ourselves.

To heap coals of fire on someone's head is a cultural tradition specific to the Orient. Someone would take burning embers from a fire that was tended to overnight and carry it in a clay pot on his head. This individual would then go from house to house and provide the means by which the rest of the village could get their fires started first thing in the morning. The phrase was used in that culture to communicate "warming someone" by your actions.

Jesus taught similar things regarding our "enemies":

Ye have heard that it hath been said, Thou shalt love thy neighbour, and hate thine enemy. But I say unto you, Love your enemies, bless them that curse you, do good to them that hate you, and pray for them which despitefully use you, and persecute you. (Matthew 5:43-44)

With all this laid out in Romans 12, the final question is how will God execute vengeance? We are told it is not ours to dish out, and that we are to love our enemies instead. Is God saying to us, "Do as I say, not as I do"? Does God not "practice what he preaches"?

The verse immediately following Matthew 5:44 has this to say:

That ye may be the children of your Father which is in heaven: for he maketh his sun to rise on the evil and on the good, and sendeth rain on the just and on the unjust. (Matthew 5:45)

It goes on to say:

*For if ye love them which love you, what reward have ye? do not even the publicans the same? And if ye salute your brethren only, what do ye more than others? do not even the publicans so? **Be ye therefore perfect, even as your Father which is in heaven is perfect**. (Matthew 5:46–48)*

No, God wants us to be like him. He loves his enemies, too. He makes the rain to fall on them as well. If we can understand the details of this subject, we can approach the perfection of love he points us to, we can be fearless, and we can have the boldness to speak the truth in love.

And we have known and believed the love that God hath to us. God is love; and he that dwelleth in love dwelleth in God, and God in him. Herein is our love made perfect, that we may have boldness in the day of judgment: because as he is, so are we in this world. There is no fear in love; but perfect love casteth out fear: because fear hath torment.

Old Testament Implications

He that feareth is not made perfect in love. (1 John 4:16–18)

In conclusion, the final verse in Romans 12 teaches us:

Be not overcome of evil, but overcome evil with good. (Romans 12:21)

This is the pathway to overcome evil and not be overcome by it. If we approach our enemies in any other way, we run the risk of being overcome by the evil that was directed toward us.

Once again, in the following record from Isaiah, the concept of vengeance focuses on what God will do for us, as opposed to what he would do to our enemies:

*Say to them that are of a fearful heart, Be strong, fear not: behold, your God will come with **vengeance**, even God with a **recompence**; he will come and save you. Then the eyes of the blind shall be opened, and the ears of the deaf shall be unstopped. Then shall the lame man leap as an hart, and the tongue of the dumb sing: for in the wilderness shall waters break out, and streams in the desert. And the parched ground shall become a pool, and the thirsty land springs of water: in* *the habitation of dragons, where each lay, shall be grass with reeds and rushes. And an highway shall be there, and a way, and it shall be called The way of holiness; the unclean shall not pass over it; but it shall be for those: the wayfaring men, though fools, shall not err therein. No lion shall be there, nor any ravenous beast shall go up thereon, it shall not be found there; but the redeemed shall walk there: And the ransomed of the* L<small>ORD</small> *shall return, and come to Zion with songs and everlasting joy upon their heads: they shall obtain joy and gladness, and sorrow and sighing shall flee away. (Isaiah 35:4–10)*

God is going to make everything right. The Savior of the world will return and pay mankind back for everything that was stolen by the enemy kingdom. That is the execution of right and justice, and the maintenance of it will be experienced when he restores paradise to his creation.

---

*Figures of Speech Used in the Bible, page 823.
**A Critical Lexicon and Concordance to the English and Greek New Testament, page 845.
***The Companion Bible, Appendix 118 2.a.

3

Judgment

SO FAR, WE have laid out the premise that God's love is a critical component in pursuing biblical accuracy on any subject in the Word of God, and that our comprehension can be flawed by our failure to live love to the fullest. Yet God, knowing our flaws, simply and comprehensively laid out the parameters of love in his Word and demonstrated them in the life of his only begotten Son. Furthermore, we looked at how the Old Testament scripture on the subject factors in, but God revealed that this was a veiled perspective and therefore not the proper viewpoint to support any structure of spiritual truth.

If these statements are true, then it logically follows that men and God judge differently. This I believe to be the truth.

> *But with me it is a very small thing that I should be judged of you, or of man's judgment: yea, I judge not mine own self. For I know nothing by myself; yet am I not hereby justified: but he that judgeth me is the Lord. Therefore judge nothing before the time, until the Lord come, who both will bring to*

light the hidden things of darkness, and will make manifest the counsels of the hearts: and then shall every man have praise of God. (1 Corinthians 4:3–5)

Here we are told, even commanded, not to judge but to leave it up to the Lord. And in case we have any question as to the extent, we are exhorted to judge NOTHING before the time. Not a thing. It is also interesting to note that the judgment of the Lord to come results in "every man having praise of God."

In this context, consider the message Jesus gave the first century church to declare:

And he commanded us to preach unto the people, and to testify that it is he which was ordained of God to be the Judge of quick and dead. (Acts 10:42)

What would his intent have been in giving them this message as their focus? Was it to instill fear? That certainly would not have been in line with the "Gospel" or "Good News" he was known for in his preaching. Hadn't Jesus had earned a reputation of being forgiving? While it was true that he did not give sinners a pass, his goal was to help them recognize, admit to, and repent from sin and therefore receive forgiveness.

Judgment

If we confess our sins, he is faithful and just to forgive us our sins, and to cleanse us from all unrighteousness. (1 John 1:9)

One of the clearest examples is found in the 8th chapter of John. This is the record of the woman taken in adultery that many believe was Mary Magdalene:

And early in the morning he came again into the temple, and all the people came unto him; and he sat down, and taught them. And the scribes and Pharisees brought unto him a woman taken in adultery; and when they had set her in the midst, They say unto him, Master, this woman was taken in adultery, in the very act. Now Moses in the law commanded us, that such should be stoned: but what sayest thou? This they said, tempting him, that they might have to accuse him. But Jesus stooped down, and with his finger wrote on the ground, as though he heard them not. (John 8:2-6)

Why did they use this particular situation to try to trap Jesus? The only logical answer would be that he had earned a reputation of being extremely forgiving. They figured they had him cornered, because this woman was undeniably a sinner who had violated the law. In the King James Version, it says they caught her "in the very act."

This was an "open and shut case," she was guilty, and there were witnesses. The root of the Greek word used in this phrase carries the meaning of "self-detected," which adds additional insight: she was honest about the sin and not covering it up. They had her "dead to rights."

And yet we know how the story turned out. The religious leaders of the time had their idea of how judgment should be carried out. She was a sinner and deserved death as the punishment according to the Old Testament law of Moses. But Jesus taught them the true intent behind that law and led them to a New Testament understanding:

> *So when they continued asking him, he lifted up himself, and said unto them, He that is without sin among you, let him first cast a stone at her. And again he stooped down, and wrote on the ground. And they which heard it, being convicted by their own conscience, went out one by one, beginning at the eldest, even unto the last: and Jesus was left alone, and the woman standing in the midst. When Jesus had lifted up himself, and saw none but the woman, he said unto her, Woman, where are those thine accusers? hath no man condemned thee? She said, No man, Lord. And Jesus said unto her, Neither do I condemn thee: go, and sin no more. (John 8:7–11)*

Judgment

Man's way of dealing with sin is different from God's. Beyond that, man's way doesn't get the job done, as we have seen in James 1:20. Jesus agreed with the accusers in theory, but then he shone the spotlight on them: "Whichever of you is without sin, go ahead and throw the first stone." And what happened? They were all convicted in their hearts and left. The only one who could have cast a stone lived in the place of perfect love, so he had a different perspective from those who were still dealing with sin themselves.

How do you think the adulteress felt? She was led to Jesus by the religious authorities and probably figured that she would be punished and put to death. Yet Jesus saved her, and his display of love and forgiveness no doubt changed her life. He told her to go and sin no more, knowing that this experience would inspire her to follow him and dwell in the darkness no longer. And if this was Mary Magdalene, as many believe, the record bears that out.

That is a very clear record of how Jesus dealt with sin in the Gospels. So, is he going to change at some point in the future?

Jesus Christ the same yesterday, and to day, and for ever. (Hebrews 13:8)

The way Jesus dealt with confessed sin in the past is the way he deals with it now and will deal with it in the future. But what about certain verses in the New Testament that seem to contradict this truth? In the same Gospel, just five chapters earlier, Jesus is recorded as saying:

He that believeth on him is not condemned: but **he that believeth not is condemned already,** *because he hath not believed in the name of the only begotten Son of God. (John 3:18)*

This verse, as it stands alone, seems to indicate that there is condemnation to the unbeliever already, right now. Then we will throw in the words "to hell" after the word condemned, because it makes us feel better. But isn't this the same angle the accusers took back in John 8?

Whenever we take a verse out of its context, we are likely to misinterpret its meaning. It is interesting that the prior verse contradicts that rendering:

For God sent not his Son into the world to condemn the world; but that the world through him might be saved. (John 3:17)

Jesus' mission on earth was not to condemn but to save. Did he forget that somehow? Many would like to believe so when we are talking about the sins of others.

But how thankful we are in the quiet places of our hearts when we too, like the accusers in John 8, reflect upon our own sins.

So how do you explain the apparent contradiction? The verses following explain the meaning:

> **And this is the condemnation**, *that light is come into the world, and men loved darkness rather than light, because their deeds were evil. For every one that doeth evil hateth the light, neither cometh to the light, lest his deeds should be reproved. But he that doeth truth cometh to the light, that his deeds may be made manifest, that they are wrought in God. (John 3:19–21)*

Right now, at this point, those who do not believe in the name of the Lord have demonstrated that they love darkness rather than light. That is the condemnation or judgment at this point. The words "condemned" and "condemnation" in this section of scripture are derivatives of the same Greek word, which more accurately carries the meaning of "judged" and "judgment." They are judged at this point, and the judgment is that they have chosen the things of this world over the things of God. They do not want to be exposed, so they hide in the dark.

Now comes the pivotal question: Is there a time limit to when sins can be confessed and repented of and forgiveness granted? Is it, as most believe, at the end of this earthly existence? Is it true that if you don't confess your sins before you die, you are going to hell and nothing can stop it?

In my many years of studying this topic, I have yet to find a verse that says that anywhere. As a matter of fact, there are many verses to the contrary, but I will address those in the later chapters of the book. Does God's mercy at some point fail and the justice men believe should come get dealt out? I will leave you with the following for your consideration:

*O give thanks unto the Lord; for he is good: for **his mercy endureth for ever**. (Psalm 136:1)*

And this is an Old Testament scripture! Well, some might say, "That is only one verse, and there are many others that speak differently."

*O give thanks unto the God of gods: for **his mercy endureth for ever**. (Psalm 136:2)*

There it is a second time, it is now confirmed and established. Oh, and by the way, there are twenty-six verses in this Psalm, and EVERY SINGLE ONE ENDS with that same phrase. God is making a point emphatically, His mercy will never end:

Judgment

O give thanks unto the Lord; *for he is good: for **his mercy endureth for ever**.*

*O give thanks unto the God of gods: for **his mercy endureth for ever**.*

*O give thanks to the Lord of lords: for **his mercy endureth for ever**.*

*To him who alone doeth great wonders: for **his mercy endureth for ever**.*

*To him that by wisdom made the heavens: for **his mercy endureth for ever**.*

*To him that stretched out the earth above the waters: for **his mercy endureth for ever**.*

*To him that made great lights: for **his mercy endureth for ever**:*

*The sun to rule by day: for **his mercy endureth for ever**:*

*The moon and stars to rule by night: for **his mercy endureth for ever**.*

*To him that smote Egypt in their firstborn: for **his mercy endureth for ever**:*

*And brought out Israel from among them: for **his mercy endureth for ever**:*

*With a strong hand, and with a stretched out arm: for **his mercy endureth for ever**.*

*To him which divided the Red sea into parts: for **his mercy endureth for ever**:*

*And made Israel to pass through the midst of it: for **his mercy endureth for ever**:*

*But overthrew Pharaoh and his host in the Red sea: for **his mercy endureth for ever**.*
*To him which led his people through the wilderness: for **his mercy endureth for ever**.*
*To him which smote great kings: for **his mercy endureth for ever**:*
*And slew famous kings: for **his mercy endureth for ever**:*
*Sihon king of the Amorites: for **his mercy endureth for ever**:*
*And Og the king of Bashan: for **his mercy endureth for ever**:*
*And gave their land for an heritage: for **his mercy endureth for ever**:*
*Even an heritage unto Israel his servant: for **his mercy endureth for ever**.*
*Who remembered us in our low estate: for **his mercy endureth for ever**:*
*And hath redeemed us from our enemies: for **his mercy endureth for ever**.*
*Who giveth food to all flesh: for **his mercy endureth for ever**.*
*O give thanks unto the God of heaven: for **his mercy endureth for ever**.*
(Psalm 136)

4

Defining Wrath

NOW IT IS time to address the term "wrath." This term immediately brings to mind a certain meaning to most everyone. If you asked 100 people on the street to define that term, you would probably get similar responses from each and every one. In fact, the *Merriam-Webster Dictionary* defines it this way:

1: Strong vengeful anger or indignation.
2: Retributory punishment for an offense or a crime: divine chastisement.

As you can see in the second definition, it is inherently associated with God. Was this the original meaning of the word, or has it been influenced by the Dark Ages and man's experience? In *Vine's Expository Dictionary of New Testament Words*, one of the main Greek words translated "wrath" in the Bible, ***orge***, is defined in the following way:

> ***Originally*** *any natural impulse, or desire, or disposition,* ***came to*** *signify anger, as the strongest of all passions.**

This word did not always mean anger, but it originally meant any natural impulse desire or disposition. It became synonymous with anger because it is believed to be the strongest of all passions. While that may be true of man, is it also true of God? Is God's strongest passion anger, or is there another passion he is best known for?

> *For God **so loved** the world, that he gave his only begotten Son, that whosoever believeth in him should not perish, but have everlasting life. (John 3:16)*

A case can be made that this is the most widely recognized scripture in the Bible. Notice that it doesn't just say that God "loved the world" but that he "SO loved the world." We use this same figure of speech when we want to emphasize our love: "I SO love you." Is it possible that the strongest of all God's passions is love?

In *Thayer's Greek Definitions*, "wrath" is described as follows:

> *To teem, denoting an internal motion, especially that of plants and fruits swelling with juice.* ***In***

Defining Wrath

> ***Greek writings from Hesiod down*** *"the natural disposition, temper, character; movement or agitation of soul, impulse, desire, any violent emotion" but especially **(and chiefly in Attic)** anger.***

Once again, we see that the original meaning of the word changed over time. Originally, the word meant to "teem as a plant" or "fruit swelling with juice." This word was changed by Hesiod and Attic to denote other things, once again defining the term based on human experience. What teems and swells in mankind in the face of opposition is not the same as what teems and swells in the heavenly Father who so loved the world that he gave his only begotten Son.

Strong's Exhaustive Concordance to the Bible provides the following etymology for ***orge***:

> *From **oregomai;** properly, desire (as a reaching forth or excitement of the mind), i.e. **(by analogy)**, violent passion (ire, or (justifiable) abhorrence); **by implication**—anger, indignation, vengeance, wrath.*

Once again, the original meaning of the word is changed to fit with man's experience. The original root word had the meaning of desire, as a reaching forth or excitement of the mind. Then by analogy and implication, the word is redefined. Once again, John 3:16 gives us an apt description of God's great desire.

Oregomai, the root word, is defined in *Strong's* this way:

> *3713 orégomai ("a primitive verb," NAS Dictionary) – properly, stretch towards; (figuratively) strongly inclined to (pulled towards); aspire to; desire to attain (acquire), reach to.*
>
> *3713 /orégomai ("aspire, stretch towards") is always in the Greek middle voice meaning, "stretching oneself out." This emphasizes the personal desire of the subject, focusing on what the object personally means to the subject (cf. Vine/ Unger, White, NT).*
>
> *[J. Thayer, "The middle voice literally means 'to stretch oneself out in order to touch or grasp something.'"]****

What is God stretching himself out to touch or grasp? What is his desire, his great passion, that has been teeming up and swelling in him? The following passage from E.W. Kenyon's book, *The Father and His Family*, illustrates it best:

Defining Wrath

Before the morning stars sang their anthem to the heart of the lonely father God, before the foundations of the earth were laid, before the first rays of light ever passed through the dark expanse, the heart of the great Creator God had a yearning, deep, mighty, eternal. It was the primordial passion for children. The father heart of the creator God longed for sons and daughters. This yearning passion took form, and God planned the universe for his man, and in the heart of that universe he purposed a home. There is no time with God. Time belongs to day and night, to sun and moon. The omnipotent God was not hampered by days, nor nights, nor years. When Love laid the foundations of this mighty universe, He planned, He purposed it all to be the home of His man. It was to be man's birthplace, man's garden of delight, man's University where he would learn to know his Father God.****

All that being noted, let's now turn to the Word of God and let the Bible define this term:

*What if God, willing to shew **his wrath**, and to make his power known, endured with much longsuffering the vessels of wrath fitted to destruction. (Romans 9:22)*

Here, "wrath" is defined in the context of who it belongs to. As we have seen from James, "The **wrath of man** worketh not the righteousness of God." A study of this word shows you that there is a wrath as it pertains to the devil appearing in the Bible as well. But the wrath of God is shown by him enduring with "much **longsuffering** the vessels of wrath fitted to destruction."

This verse is critical in our understanding of God's intense passion, so we'll take the time to break it down in more detail.

First of all, let's look at the term "vessels of wrath." A look at the overall context makes it clear that this is referring to a category of human beings:

> *What if God, willing to shew his wrath, and to make his power known, endured with much longsuffering the vessels of wrath fitted to destruction: And that he might make known the riches of his glory on the vessels of mercy, which he had afore prepared unto glory. (Romans 9:22–23)*

There are two distinct categories listed here: vessels of wrath fitted to destruction and vessels of mercy prepared unto glory. This dichotomy runs the length of the entire Word of God and will be explored in detail in the coming chapters. For now, we will look at the vessels of wrath

Defining Wrath

fitted to destruction. Who is this referring to? Again, we turn to the pages of the Bible to define its own terms:

> *Let no man deceive you with vain words: for because of these things cometh the **wrath of God** upon the **children of disobedience**. (Ephesians 5:6)*

> *For which things' sake the **wrath of God** cometh on the **children of disobedience**. (Colossians 3:6)*

It is established that the "wrath of God" is coming upon the "children of disobedience." These are the "vessels of wrath," and later on we will be developing this subject further. This is the one group of humans that has been standing in the way of God's great desire to be with humanity. They will find themselves on the wrong side of the passion teeming inside of God to reunite with mankind. Just imagine your child was being held by a kidnapper, and you had a chance to save him and the means to do so. Your passion and love for your child would have a negative impact on the captor. There is more to say on this subject, and several future chapters will be dedicated to it.

> *Wherein in time past ye walked according to the course of this world, according to the prince of the*

power of the air, the spirit that now worketh in the **children of disobedience**. *(Ephesians 2:2)*

These "children of disobedience" are the ones in whom the prince of the power of the air works to set the courses of the world, which lead people away from God.

For the **wrath of God** *is revealed from heaven against all ungodliness and unrighteousness* **of** *men, who hold the truth in unrighteousness. (Romans 1:18)*

It is intriguing that this verse, in the opening section of the revelation to us in this day and time, addresses the wrath of God. One very small word with a very large meaning is used in this context: **OF**. God's wrath is directed at the ungodliness and unrighteousness **OF** the men who hold or suppress the truth. Once again, he wants to remove all the obstacles that stand in the way of the desire of his heart. Exactly how this all plays out will be addressed later in the book.

For now, the point is to see that God's intense passion is displayed by the longsuffering he extends to these people. The word "longsuffering" here in Romans is exactly the same one used in 1 Corinthians to describe love. As a matter of fact, it is the very first descriptive word used there:

> *Charity **suffereth long**, and is kind; charity envieth not; charity vaunteth not itself, is not puffed up. (1 Corinthians 13:4)*

Putting this all together, God's great passion and desire is to be with mankind once again and was most clearly demonstrated by the long suffering love he manifested toward those who stand in the way of it's fulfillment. We already know that He will succeed in His endeavor, and that reunion is recorded in the second half of Revelation 20 through the end of the Bible. He sent his Son to pave the way for that event, and the purpose of his ministry was reflected in the name he was given in Isaiah and referred to in Matthew:

> *Behold, a virgin shall be with child, and shall bring forth a son, and they shall call his name **Emmanuel**, which being interpreted is, **God with us**. (Matthew 1:23)*

In summary, these first four chapters were intended to lay the groundwork and foundation for the rest of the book. There are so many other scriptures that could have been used to support these premises, but for the sake of brevity, I have chosen only the ones that I believe best represent the truths set forth. You are highly exhorted to consider these things yourself and to search the matter in the Bible as the Bereans spoken of in Acts:

*These were more **noble** than those in Thessalonica, in that they received the word with all readiness of mind, and searched the scriptures daily, whether those things were so. (Acts 17:11)*

I believe that the best way to describe the biblical teachings on the future is by using the analogy of a puzzle box. There is no question that there are lots of pieces all over the Word of God on the subject. Whole books of the Bible are dedicated to it, and our Lord spoke much about it. Then why is there still so much confusion and so little really understood on the topic?

Could it be we have been looking at the wrong puzzle box? When putting a jigsaw puzzle together with the pieces spread out all over the table, the first thing we do is look at the picture on the box to get perspective. We can see what the picture should look like when all the pieces are placed properly. In that context, we can see what pieces should go where by looking at their colors, shapes, etc.

What if we were looking at the wrong box? I believe the picture of an angry God taking his wrath out on mankind is from the wrong puzzle box, so all the pieces we have don't fit together. It is my belief that with the correct overall picture set before you in these first four chapters, all the scriptures in the Word of God will fit and the picture of the future will become clearer.

As with a puzzle, generally the first part that gets completed is the perimeter of the picture. That has been my goal up to this point. Now it is time to go into the scriptures regarding future events to see if they fit with what we have set so far.

Vine's Expository Dictionary of New Testament Words, page 57.
**Thayer's Greek Definitions*, Electronic Database. Copyright © 2002, 2003, 2006, 2011 by Biblesoft, Inc. All rights reserved. Used by permission. BibleSoft.com.
***https://Biblehub.com/greek/3709.htm
****Kenyon, *The Father and His Family*, pp. 22–23.

5

God's Nature and Plan from the Beginning

Remember the former things of old: for I am God, and there is none else; I am God, and there is none like me, Declaring **the end from the beginning,** *and from ancient times the things that are not yet done, saying,* **My counsel shall stand, and I will do all my pleasure.** *(Isaiah 46:9–10)*

IN THE SCRIPTURE referenced above, God tells us that he has been declaring what is going to happen in the end from the very beginning. Whenever I think of this truth, I am reminded of a story a famous pastor shared on his radio broadcast. He talked about when he visited the home of a best-selling author and saw Post-it notes all over the wall. This author said that it was actually the end of the book he was working on first, and that this was his normal procedure. Once he knew how the story would end, he would then work on the rest of the book leading up to it.

How many times have you seen a movie or read a book where there is a significant twist at the end? The character we thought was the good guy turned out to be the bad guy or vice versa. The author knew that all along, and developed the narrative accordingly. If we take the time to read the book or watch the movie again, we then see the signs all along the way. The same is true of the book we refer to as the Holy Bible. When we understand the ending, how the counsel of God does stand and how he does accomplish ALL his pleasure, then we can see the clues that were there all along the way.

The first recorded prophecy in the Bible is found in Genesis chapter 3:

> *And the* Lord *God said unto the serpent, Because thou hast done this, thou art cursed above all cattle, and above every beast of the field; upon thy belly shalt thou go, and dust shalt thou eat all the days of thy life: And I will put enmity between thee and the woman, and between thy seed and her seed; it shall bruise thy head, and thou shalt bruise his heel. (Genesis 3:14–15)*

Most are familiar with the second part of verse 15, as a reference to the crucifixion and the victory that will be wrought as a result. But notice that there are two seeds mentioned: the seed of the woman who we know to be Jesus Christ, and the "seed of the serpent." Consider for now the possibility that this is referring to a group of human beings that we talked about before: the vessels of wrath fitted to destruction, the children of disobedience.

In *The Companion Bible*, E.W. Bullinger has this to say about the reference to them in Ephesians 2:2 where he defines the term "children of disobedience":

> *Hebraism: not disobedient children, but sons of Satan in a special manner, being those in whom he works, and on whom the wrath of God comes.*

This original prophecy in Genesis 3:15 tells us that the "enmity" or hatred that exists in the world:

1. Originates from the devil and was directed at the woman (who would eventually give birth to the Christ), and
2. Would be introduced into the world by way of his seed or offspring and directed at the seed of the woman and ultimately the church, which would have the seed of "Christ in them."

Notice again the dichotomy in the human realm of point number 2. The conflict between these two groups, namely the enmity of the "serpent's seed" toward the "woman's seed," is truly the source of all the hatred that has existed throughout history unto this day, and it will continue until the end of time.

Now we'll look at the context of that original prophecy to gain some more understanding and build on the foundation we have set to this point. As we all know, Adam and Eve were manipulated by the devil into committing the one sin that God had warned them about.

Let's look at the interaction between God and the two of them after that happened:

> *And the LORD God called unto Adam, and said unto him, Where art thou? And he said, I heard thy voice in the garden, and I was afraid, because I was naked; and I hid myself. (Genesis 3:9–10)*

One result of man's disobedience was fear, and we know that perfect love casts it out. No doubt the omniscient heavenly Father took note of this and built it into his plan.

> *And he said, Who told thee that thou wast naked? Hast thou eaten of the tree, whereof I commanded thee that thou shouldest not eat? And the man said, The woman whom thou gavest to be with me, she gave me of the tree, and I did eat. (Genesis 3:11–12)*

God then begins a dialogue with Adam to get to the source of the issue. Adam responds with full transparency

God's Nature and Plan from the Beginning

and confesses his sin. I used to believe that he was passing the blame when he told God that it was the woman who caused him to fall. Furthermore, it looks as though he's reminding God that he gave the woman to be with him, in a sense indirectly blaming God as well. I no longer believe that to be the case. This is just an honest confession of what happened followed by an absolute admission of his sin: "I did eat."

Once again, the record in 1 John tells us that he is forgiven. This truth is the way God has always operated, and therefore it applies here.

> *If we confess our sins, he is faithful and just to forgive us our sins, and to cleanse us from all unrighteousness. (1 John 1:9)*

Adam is forgiven. Now God directs his attention toward Eve:

> *And the LORD God said unto the woman, What is this that thou hast done? And the woman said, The serpent beguiled me, and I did eat. (Genesis 3:13)*

This again is nothing more than an "out and out" confession. Later, 2 Corinthians 11:3 uses very similar wording when referring to this event: "The serpent beguiled Eve through his subtilty." She was tricked and also confessed that she "did eat."

So by the end of verse 13, both Adam and Eve are forgiven. Now God directs his attention and focus on the deceiver:

> *And the* Lord *God said unto the serpent,* **Because thou hast done this**, *thou art cursed above all cattle, and above every beast of the field; upon thy belly shalt thou go, and dust shalt thou eat all the days of thy life. (Genesis 3:14)*

God lays the blame for the fall of mankind solely on the serpent. God has not changed his opinion in the matter since. He does not blame mankind for what the devil does. Instead, he has figured out a way to save humanity from this precarious situation without violating his nature of love or free will. The beauty of how he does this is recorded in the Bible:

> *He hath not dealt with us after our sins, nor rewarded us according to our iniquities. For as the heaven is high above the earth, so great is his mercy toward them that fear him. As far as the east is from the west, so far hath he removed our transgressions from us. Like as a father pitieth his children, so the Lord pitieth them that fear him.*

God's Nature and Plan from the Beginning

For he knoweth our frame; he remembereth that we are dust. (Psalm 103:10–14)

I would like to also draw your attention to one other thing in Genesis 3:14: the pronouncement of a curse upon the serpent. Keep this in mind as we continue moving forward in this record:

And the Lord *God said unto the serpent, Because thou hast done this, thou art* **cursed** *above all cattle, and above every beast of the field; upon thy belly shalt thou go, and dust shalt thou eat all the days of thy life. (Genesis 3:14)*

Even though mankind is forgiven, there are consequences now to his disobedience. Evil has now entered into God's creation, and there will be an impact upon it as a result:

Unto the woman he said, I will greatly multiply thy sorrow and thy conception; in sorrow thou shalt bring forth children; and thy desire shall be to thy husband, and he shall rule over thee. And unto Adam he said, Because thou hast hearkened unto the voice of thy wife, and hast eaten of the tree, of which I commanded thee, saying, Thou shalt not eat of it: **cursed** *is the ground for thy* *sake; in sorrow shalt thou eat of it all the days of thy life; Thorns also and thistles shall it bring forth to thee; and thou shalt eat the herb of the field; In the sweat of thy face shalt thou eat bread, till thou return unto the ground; for out of it wast thou taken: for dust thou art, and unto dust shalt thou return. (Genesis 3:16–19)*

Note that in verse 17, the ground also is now cursed. The Hebrew word used for "ground" is also translated "earth." So now we have two things that are cursed, the serpent and the earth. And one thing they both have in common is that they will not continue into the glorious eternity called paradise that God has prepared for his children.

A few verses later comes a section of scripture that is very significant to our study:

And the Lord God said, Behold, the man is become as one of us, to know good and evil: and now, lest he put forth his hand, and take also of the tree of life, and eat, and live for ever: Therefore the Lord God sent him forth from the garden of Eden, to till the ground from whence he was taken. So he drove out the man; and he placed at the east of the garden of Eden Cherubims, and a flaming

God's Nature and Plan from the Beginning

sword which turned every way, to keep the way of the tree of life. (Genesis 3:22-24)

The terminology used in verse 24 is pretty direct: God drove man out of the garden. The word "drove" carries a very clear meaning of force being applied. This appears to be the closest God ever came to overstepping the free will of man. What was God's grave concern?

Verse 22 ends with the figure of speech *aposiopesis*, which indicates "sudden silence."* The narrative stops abruptly, implying that the results of the preceding activity would be "unspeakable." If Adam and Eve were to eat from the Tree of Life at this point and "live forever" in their yet unredeemed state, they would remain in that fallen condition throughout eternity. That fate is unthinkable to God who so desires with the greatest of passion to spend all of eternity with mankind.

As we will see in the next chapter, there are some that do choose this destiny, even though our loving God does everything he can to dissuade that choice without overstepping their free will. This is the pathway for a human to become "seed of the serpent," as we will continue to unveil in the pages to come.

---

*Figures of Speech Used in the Bible, E.W. Bullinger, pp. 151–152.

6

Cain

THE DICHOTOMY RESUMES as we continue in the book of Genesis, where we find another sin committed and God's intervention. However, this time the response and outcome are very different:

> *And Adam knew Eve his wife; and she conceived, and bare Cain, and said, I have gotten a man from the* LORD. *And she again bare his brother Abel. And Abel was a keeper of sheep, but Cain was a tiller of the ground. And in process of time it came to pass, that Cain brought of the fruit of the ground an offering unto the* LORD. *And Abel, he also brought of the firstlings of his flock and of the fat thereof. And the* LORD *had respect unto Abel and to his offering: But unto Cain and to his offering he had not respect. And Cain was very wroth, and his countenance fell. (Genesis 4:1–5)*

In this record, we see that God intervenes even before Cain kills his brother Abel. God is trying to work with him while the sin is in the incubation stage in his mind.

And the LORD said unto Cain, Why art thou wroth? and why is thy countenance fallen? If thou doest well, shalt thou not be accepted? and if thou doest not well, sin lieth at the door. And unto thee shall be his desire, and thou shalt rule over him. (Genesis 4:6–7)

Cain does not respond to God's intercession in any way at all. We might even wonder about the retention of his vocal abilities until we see in the next verse that they remain intact:

And Cain talked with Abel his brother: and it came to pass, when they were in the field, that Cain rose up against Abel his brother, and slew him. (Genesis 4:8)

Even after the fact, God engages him in the hope that it might elicit a confession as he was able to with his parents earlier. Yet Cain dodges the question altogether and proves that he has no intention of taking responsibility for his sin.

And the LORD said unto Cain, Where is Abel thy brother? And he said, I know not: Am I my brother's keeper? (Genesis 4:9)

God has done everything he could to redirect Cain away from the fate he has chosen. Although this record spans only several verses in the Bible, no doubt these events transpired over a lengthier period of time than it may seem. God started reaching out to him from the time he began to consider the lies of the deceiver, but Cain would not have anything to do with it. The behavior demonstrated in verses 6 and 7 reveal the depth of his commitment to the Evil One, even before the murder took place.

God's mercy and longsuffering are displayed in how he still engages Cain after he killed Abel, yet Cain exhibits no remorse whatsoever. His commitment to lawlessness coupled with his unwillingness to confess and repent result in the very thing God drove Adam and Eve out of paradise to prevent. The deeper truth here is that Cain made a choice with eternal ramifications that will exclude him from God's plan of the future. He has given total allegiance to the serpent in his mind and his actions, and in so doing, he made him lord of his life. He is the first "seed of the serpent," and God's response in verse 10 makes this plain:

*And he said, What hast thou done? the voice of thy brother's blood crieth unto me from the ground. And now art thou **cursed** from the earth, which hath opened her mouth to receive thy brother's* *blood from thy hand; When thou tillest the ground, it shall not henceforth yield unto thee her strength; a fugitive and a vagabond shalt thou be in the earth. (Genesis 4:10–12)*

God declares that Cain is now cursed, and the original text carries the idea of "above the earth" instead of "from." The curse he brought upon himself was through intentional and deliberate acts of disobedience, even though God sought to save him. He is now cursed along with the serpent and the earth, indicating that his destiny will be the same: exclusion from the presence of God in the future. This breaks God's heart.

The next verse is very revealing:

And Cain said unto the LORD, My punishment is greater than I can bear. (Genesis 4:13)

The statement "My punishment is greater than I can bear" in seven of the ancient texts, along with the writings of Greek and Latin fathers, is actually a question translated: "Is mine iniquity too great to be forgiven?" He was obviously made aware of the interaction between the Lord and his parents, and this question was more likely a snide remark than an actual heartfelt query. Because he made a commitment with eternal ramifications in an unredeemed state, the answer is "Yes."

Could this be what Jesus referred to as the blasphemy against the Holy Ghost?

> *Wherefore I say unto you, All manner of sin and blasphemy shall be forgiven unto men: but the blasphemy against the Holy Ghost shall not be forgiven unto men. And whosoever speaketh a word against the Son of man, it shall be forgiven him: but whosoever speaketh against the Holy Ghost,* **it shall not be forgiven him***, neither in this world, neither in the world to come. (Matthew 12:31-32)*

This would be the one and only sin that is unforgiveable. It is not because God is unwilling to forgive it, but because the sinner is unwilling to repent, and the deal is sealed by the presence of seed. Just like his father the devil, Cain has no intention of changing his mind. He has made an absolute commitment to darkness, so he will share in its destiny in the future.

This is not something that a person stumbles into during a "wild night out with the boys." This takes contemplation, consideration, and commitment over a long period of time with eyes wide open, knowing exactly who and what one is selling out to. And just as God did with Cain, and even earlier with Adam and Eve when he drove them out of the garden, he does everything he can to dissuade this choice. But because love requires free will, this choice is on the table and there are some that will make it.

What happens next is extraordinary and brings us back to a truth covered earlier:

> *Behold, thou hast driven me out this day from the face of the earth; and from thy face shall I be hid; and I shall be a fugitive and a vagabond in the earth; and it shall come to pass, that every one that findeth me shall slay me. And the* Lord *said unto him, Therefore whosoever slayeth Cain, vengeance shall be taken on him sevenfold. And the* Lord *set a mark upon Cain, lest any finding him should kill him. And Cain went out from the presence of the* Lord, *and dwelt in the land of Nod, on the east of Eden. (Genesis 4:14–16)*

Cain somehow knows that everyone would be out to kill him now that he has aligned himself with the serpent, and he asks for God's help. As shocking as that might seem, what is even more surprising is God's response. God protects him—one who has committed himself to God's archenemy and totally rejected him. This is the first example and a clear illustration of what is recorded in Romans 9:

What if God, willing to shew his wrath, and to make his power known, **endured with much longsuffering the vessels of wrath fitted to destruction.** *(Romans 9:22)*

God's response to Cain's request *after* he sells out to the devil is the greatest display of God's *unconditional* love to the greatest possible degree, which is the point this verse is making. What better way to illustrate that absolute fullness of his great passion than to see it in action in the life of an eternally committed foe. When God tells us to love even our enemies, he is not expecting us to do something that he himself hasn't already done more times than we may ever fully comprehend.

God also sets Cain apart with a "mark" in verse 15. This will come up again as we study those who commit the blasphemy against the Holy Ghost. The seed of the serpent. The children of disobedience. The cursed children. These alone are the ones upon whom the wrath of God will have a negative impact, which we will develop going forward.

In God's first interaction with mankind regarding sin, Adam and Eve repent and confess, and they are forgiven. They represent the "vessels of mercy prepared unto glory" in Romans 9:23. Then there is Cain, who does not repent nor confess and so represents the "vessels of wrath fitted to destruction." This builds on top of the prophecy in Genesis 3:15 as the theme from there all the way to Revelation, as we will see in the next chapter.

> *Not as Cain, who was **of** that wicked one, and slew his brother. And wherefore slew he him? Because his own works were evil, and his brother's righteous. (1 John 3:12)*

7

The Judgments

WE ARE READY now to take our first foray into the book of Revelation. I feel it necessary to address the concern that is voiced many times when looking into this section of the Word of God. This was a theology I espoused also in the past. "It is not available for us to know the things concerning the future." And then the following verse will be quoted:

> *But as it is written, Eye hath not seen, nor ear heard, neither have entered into the heart of man, the things which God hath prepared for them that love him. (1 Corinthians 2:9)*

The first five words in this verse should get our attention. "But as it is written" tells us that this is a quote from the Old Testament where it was previously written—Isaiah 64:4, to be exact. As we discussed in a previous chapter, this truth will be a veiled perspective coming out of the Old Testament and is no longer applicable in the fullest sense. The next verse elaborates:

> *But God hath revealed them unto us by his Spirit: for the Spirit searcheth all things, yea, the deep things of God. (1 Corinthians 2:10)*

"But" at the beginning of this verse ties in contrast what follows with the previous Old Testament truth. God has revealed these things to us by way of his Spirit, and these truths are the "deep things of God." God wants us to know the details of the future, and he has been telling us about it since the beginning. It was never anything that could be seen by way of the senses, as verse 9 communicates. It took the Spirit of God, which was upon some in the Old Testament and is now available to all because of the accomplished work of Jesus Christ. We can actually read about what is yet to happen, and God wants us to know.

An Old Testament truth that transcends the chasm and is applicable in this context is as follows:

> *The secret things belong unto the* LORD *our God: but those things which are revealed belong unto us and to our children for ever, that we may do all the words of this law. (Deuteronomy 29:29)*

God's intent in revealing "secret things" is so "that we may do all the words of this law" or be able to carry out his will in any day and time. In like manner, the

The Judgments

details pertaining to the future or "the deep things" he has revealed to us by way of the Spirit provide an anchor to our souls so that we can forge ahead and remain on track even during the storms of life:

That hope is real and true, an anchor to steady our restless souls, a hope that leads us back behind the curtain to where God is (as the high priests did in the days when reconciliation flowed from sacrifices in the temple). (Hebrews 6:19 The Voice)

We are going to start in the 20th chapter of the book of Revelation. While much of this book is symbolic and figurative, there is also a lot that is easy to see and gain from simply reading the text.

And I saw an angel come down from heaven, having the key of the bottomless pit and a great chain in his hand. And he laid hold on the dragon, that old serpent, which is the Devil, and Satan, and bound him a thousand years, And cast him into the bottomless pit, and shut him up, and set a seal upon him, that he should deceive the nations no more, till the thousand years should be fulfilled: and after that he must be loosed a little season. (Revelation 20:1–3)

This chapter starts out with the devil being bound and cast into a bottomless pit, where he will be shut up and unable to deceive for a period of a thousand years. Verse 2 lists four different terms used to describe him. The first one is the "dragon," which is a term referring to the devil used thirteen times in the New Testament, all of which are found in the book of Revelation. The first usage defines the term:

And there appeared another wonder in heaven; and behold a great red dragon, having seven heads and ten horns, and seven crowns upon his heads. And his tail drew the third part of the stars of heaven, and did cast them to the earth: and the dragon stood before the woman which was ready to be delivered, for to devour her child as soon as it was born. (Revelation 12:3–4)

What is clear from these two verses is the reference to the celestial signs and the battle waged against the woman. This is another reference to Genesis 3:15. These scriptures seem to indicate that the "dragon" refers to the devil's spiritual warfare in the heavenlies to stop God's plan regarding the Messiah.

The next term in Revelation 20:2 is "that old serpent," which is yet another clear reference back to the record in Genesis 3. Some texts render it "that ancient serpent" or "the serpent of old." In case there's any question whatsoever about who this is referring to, the third term makes it clear: "which is the devil."

Then comes an interesting twist. The next term used to describe the devil is prefaced with the conjunction "and," indicating an additional entity: Satan. I have heard it taught and believe it to be true that this term refers to his entire kingdom and would therefore explain the conjunction separating it. So we see that the enemy of God who battles in the heavens entered into the terrestrial realm and the affairs of mankind as a serpent (which is none other than the devil), **AND** his entire kingdom are bound for a period of a thousand years.

The reference to this period of 1,000 years is found in verses 2 through 7, emphasizing that God does not want us to miss this point. Many have drawn the conclusion that this is what is known as the "millennial kingdom." If that is the case, which I believe to be so, then we see that the enemy and his entire kingdom will be bound for the duration of it.

The next verse tells us who will be included in this kingdom:

> *And I saw thrones, and they sat upon them, and judgment was given unto them: and I saw the souls of them that were beheaded for the witness of Jesus, and for the word of God, and which had not*

> *worshipped the beast, neither his image, neither had received his mark upon their foreheads, or in their hands; and they lived and reigned with Christ a thousand years. (Revelation 20:4)*

As this verse appears in the King James Version, there are only two groups described: those doing the judging and those being judged. We learn in the next verse that everyone else will remain in the grave until after this period. Then it clearly tells us that this is the first resurrection.

> *But the rest of the dead lived not again until the thousand years were finished. This is the first resurrection. (Revelation 20:5)*

As stated before with the multiple uses of "1,000 years" in the verses describing it, it is not a huge leap to consider the possibility that the first resurrection is the millennial kingdom. If that is so, then we know that the devil and his kingdom will not be actively deceiving mankind during that time. This section of scripture is a broad overview of that period, just hitting on the major points and serving mainly to set the chronology of events happening during it. **This is the first period of "judgment" referred to many different times in the Bible.**

So the question remains: Who will be judged during this time? This question has caused much confusion throughout the ages and has given way to a multitude of answers. Again, it is important to look at the clear verses on the subject. One simple point that can be deduced and a good place to start is the fact that there are two resurrections.

Although the second resurrection is not mentioned here specifically, it is inferred by the language in verse 5. This thousand-year period is the first resurrection, and the rest of the dead will live again after it is finished. Simple math tells you that there are two resurrections.

The following two verses confirm and establish that truth:

And shall come forth; they that have done good, unto the resurrection of life; and they that have done evil, unto the resurrection of damnation. (John 5:29)

And have hope toward God, which they themselves also allow, that there shall be a resurrection of the dead, both of the just and unjust. (Acts 24:15)

In these two scriptures, the resurrections are named in terms of who will be involved in them. The first resurrection is that of life and is for the just, and the second resurrection is that of damnation and is for the unjust. Once again, we see the dichotomy we have tracked through the Word of God up to this point. Could it be that the resurrections listed in Revelation 20 coincide with the theme we have so far addressed? Is it possible that the first resurrection is for the vessels of mercy who are prepared unto glory, and the second resurrection for the vessels of wrath fitted to destruction?

Let's look a little closer at the definition of those who will be judged during the first resurrection to see if we might be on to something here:

And I saw thrones, and they sat upon them, and judgment was given unto them: and I saw the souls of them that were beheaded for the witness of Jesus, and for the word of God, and which had not worshipped the beast, neither his image, neither had received his mark upon their foreheads, or in their hands; and they lived and reigned with Christ a thousand years. (Revelation 20:4)

In the King James text, it appears that the second part of the verse refers to those to be judged. This group of people had two characteristics:

1. They were beheaded for the witness of Jesus and for the Word of God.

The Judgments

2. They had not worshiped the beast or his image and had not received his mark upon their foreheads or in their hands.

This would fit easily with the descriptions from the Gospel of John and the book of Acts in which they are described as the just who are raised unto life. Verse 6 of this chapter tells us more about these people:

Blessed and holy is he that hath part in the first resurrection: on such the second death hath no power, but they shall be priests of God and of Christ, and shall reign with him a thousand years. (Revelation 20:6)

We see also that they are blessed and holy and that the second death has no power over them.

The rest of the dead will be part of the second resurrection, which is that of the unjust unto damnation. Verse 6 therefore seems to infer that they are damned instead of blessed and unholy instead of holy, and the second death will have power over them.

So there you have it: a nice little tightly wrapped package of who is in the two resurrections.

But now we have a problem, and here is where all the hellfire and brimstone theologies kick into gear. If we go by the definition given in verse 4 of the participants in the first resurrection, it is a very exclusive group. As it is written in the King James Version, we know that they did not worship the beast or his image and did not receive the mark upon their heads or hands, and that is easy to understand. However, the first part of the description must apply as well: they were beheaded for their stands on truth.

If that is the case, we are all in a world of trouble. With that description of those in the first resurrection, we have just lost David and Moses for starters. If the text is correct and they are included in the "rest of the dead," then they will be part of the resurrection of the unjust to damnation and everything that comes along with it. If only those who were beheaded make it into the first resurrection, we have error upon error upon error. So what's the answer?

One small word in verse 4 is the difference between truth and error, and once again, it puts everything back into a perspective that fits with the rest of the Word of God. The word I am referring to is the word "which":

> And I saw thrones, and they sat upon them, and judgment was given unto them: and I saw the souls of them that were beheaded for the witness of Jesus, and for the word of God, and **which** had not worshipped the beast, neither his image, neither had received his mark upon their foreheads, or

The Judgments

in their hands; and they lived and reigned with Christ a thousand years. (Revelation 20:4)

That one word that couples the two sets of descriptions together makes it look as though it is referring to only one group. It is the word *hoitines* in the Greek texts, and it would be better translated "anyone who," "someone who," or "whoever." If this is true, it changes the passage quite profoundly and introduces a second group of participants instead of listing a second set of qualities for just the one. Many of the different versions render it this way:

And such as *worshipped not the beast. (American Standard Version)*

Also those who *had not worshipped the beast. (Complete Jewish Bible)*

And those who *had not worshiped the beast. (English Standard Version)*

And those who *had not worshiped the beast. (New American Standard Bible)*

And also those who *had not worshipped the monster. (New Testament for Everyone)*

> ***And such as*** *didn't worship the beast. (World English Bible)*

> ***And them that*** *worshipped not the beast. (Wycliffe)*

If this second set of qualities listed is indeed the introduction of a second group, then instead of the first resurrection being extremely exclusive, it is actually a very inclusive group. In other words, those participating in this millennial kingdom include those who died as martyrs, everyone who did not worship the beast, **and everyone in between.** In modern vernacular, we would say this is a list "from A to Z" or from "soup to nuts," a figurative way of communicating a very inclusive group of humanity by employing the figure of speech merismos.

If that is the correct rendering, then it can simply be said that anyone who did not worship the beast or his image and did not receive the mark on his forehead or hands would be a part of the millennial kingdom. I believe this is the correct understanding, and I will continue to build upon that premise.

There may be many thoughts running through your mind right now, and I ask you to write them down at this point. I am continuing to build my case, and I believe everything will be addressed before the end of the book. That being said, we need to answer two questions right

The Judgments

away. First, what about the true church, which consists of those who are born again since the day of Pentecost?

Jesus taught the following in that context:

Jesus answered and said unto him, Verily, verily, I say unto thee, Except a man be born again, he cannot see the kingdom of God. Jesus answered, Verily, verily, I say unto thee, Except a man be born of water and of the Spirit, he cannot enter into the kingdom of God. (John 3:3 and 5)

Based on these two scriptures, it can also be said that those who are born again **would** enter into and see the kingdom of God. Later in the same conversation with Nicodemus, Jesus stated:

That whosoever believeth in him should not perish, but have eternal life. (John 3:15)

Those who believe in Jesus are born again, already have eternal life, and will enter into and see the kingdom of God. It is a "done deal," an accomplished reality and the greatest gift of all time.

For the wages of sin is death; but the gift of God is eternal life through Jesus Christ our Lord. (Romans 6:23)

In that context, let's revisit a point set forth in Chapter 3 of this book, where we discussed that the words for "condemned" or "condemnation" are interchangeable with the words "judged" or "judgment," and that the context would determine which rendering is applicable. The renderings of "judge" and "judgment" fit best in the following scriptures and add additional light on the subject:

He that believeth on him is not condemned [judged]: *but he that believeth not is condemned [judged] already, because he hath not believed in the name of the only begotten Son of God. (John 3:18)*

Verily, verily, I say unto you, **He that heareth my word, and believeth on him that sent me,** *hath everlasting life, and* **shall not come into condemnation [judgment];** *but is passed from death unto life. (John 5:24)*

There is therefore now no condemnation [judgment] to them which are in Christ Jesus, *who walk not after the flesh, but after the Spirit. (Romans 8:1)*

The Judgments

Born-again believers already have eternal life, and therefore they will not go through the judgment, which is the first resurrection. We will already be gathered together with the Lord prior to this and will return with him at the beginning of the millennial kingdom. (I will provide a chronology of those events as I believe they will unfold later for your consideration.)

This particular subject would require an entire book to cover in depth, and it is not the purpose of this study. On that note, however, if someone does not agree with the "once saved always saved" concept of the New Testament, but has not committed the "blasphemy against the Holy Ghost," he can feel free to put himself into the first resurrection and find great comfort there as the rest of the study unfolds.

> *And this is the record, that God hath given to us eternal life, and this life is in his Son. These things have I written unto you that believe on the name of the Son of God; that ye may know that ye have eternal life, and that ye may believe on the name of the Son of God. (1 John 5:11 and 13)*

If all of this is true, then the following question remains: Who are the participants in the second resurrection? Who are the "rest of the dead" spoken of in Revelation 20:5? The answer is quite simple: those who

DID worship the beast or its image and who **DID** receive the mark on their foreheads or hands. We will explore this conclusion in the next chapter.

8

Resurrection of the Unjust

I WILL SET aside a whole chapter to discuss this topic. Among other things, I want to make it clear that you are not going to be part of this group. This refers to a relatively small number of individuals at any point in history who have completely sold out to the devil and will not listen to anything God has to say, as already demonstrated in the record of the prototype Cain. The mere fact that you are reading this book and are considering the message shows that you are not in this category. And if you have the proof of being born again, you are sealed with the Holy Spirit of promise, so it is impossible for you to receive a second "eternal spirit"; you are going to be a part of God's plan for the future, and nothing can change that.

The first quality from Revelation 20:4 we are going to track is the "mark":

> *And I saw thrones, and they sat upon them, and judgment was given unto them: and I saw the souls of them that were beheaded for the witness of Jesus, and for the word of God, and which had not*

*worshipped the beast, neither his image, neither had received his **mark** upon their foreheads, or in their hands; and they lived and reigned with Christ a thousand years.*

In a previous chapter, we looked at the record of Cain from Genesis chapter 4; he was the first human to receive the "mark":

And the L<small>ORD</small> *said unto him, Therefore whosoever slayeth Cain, vengeance shall be taken on him sevenfold. And the* L<small>ORD</small> *set a **mark** upon Cain, lest any finding him should kill him. (Genesis 4:15)*

Cain rejected all of God's attempts to redirect him from his commitment to evil. Again, this most likely took place over a longer period of time than the short record in the Bible might suggest. Cain would have moved forward in his commitment, fully knowing who God was and what his will for his life would be, as well who the devil was and what his plans were. This selling out to the devil resulted in his receiving the "seed of the serpent" and becoming his son:

*We are none of us to have the spirit of Cain, who was a **son** of the devil and murdered his brother. Have you realised his motive? It was just because* *he realised the goodness of his brother's life and the rottenness of his own. (1 John 3:12, J.B. Phillips New Testament)*

The "mark" he received is synonymous with his being a "son of the devil." This is said in another way in verse 11 when God pronounced his "judgment":

*And now art thou **cursed** from the earth, which hath opened her mouth to receive thy brother's blood from thy hand. (Genesis 4:11)*

Cain, who received the mark and was referred to as a child of the devil, is also a cursed one, which fits with the record in Revelation 20. He will not be part of the first resurrection, which is for the "blessed and holy," seeing he is "cursed" and therefore "unholy."

*Having eyes full of adultery, and that cannot cease from sin; beguiling unstable souls: an heart they have exercised with covetous practices; **cursed** children. (2 Peter 2:14)*

The immediate context in the same verse reveals some additional insights into these "cursed ones." Their "eyes are FULL of adultery," and they "CANNOT cease from sin." In the greater context of the chapter in 2 Peter, we learn the following as well:

> *But there were false prophets also among the people, even as there shall be false teachers among you, who privily shall bring in damnable heresies, even denying the Lord that bought them, and bring upon themselves swift **destruction**. (2 Peter 2:1)*

They are the "vessels of wrath fitted to destruction" of Romans 9.

> *The Lord knoweth how to deliver the godly out of temptations, and to reserve **the unjust** unto the day of judgment to be punished. (2 Peter 2:9)*

They are the "unjust" of the second resurrection. And instead of being "prepared unto glory" as the vessels of mercy, there destiny is more bleak:

> *These are wells without water, clouds that are carried with a tempest; **to whom the mist of darkness** is reserved for ever. (2 Peter 2:17)*

Another interesting tie in can be found in the book of Jude, where it describes these individuals in similar fashion and language:

> *Woe unto them! for **they have gone in the way of Cain**, and ran greedily after the error of Balaam for reward, and perished in the gainsaying of Core. These are spots in your feasts of charity, when they feast with you, feeding themselves without fear: clouds they are without water, carried about of winds; trees whose fruit withereth, without fruit, **twice dead**, plucked up by the roots. (Jude 11–12)*

The second death WILL have power over them. How clear could it be?

Jesus addressed them shortly after forgiving the woman taken in adultery. The scribes and Pharisees who brought her to Jesus learned the lesson he was sharing and left the scene, being convicted in their own hearts. However, there were some who remained, who had a real problem with his display of mercy:

> *Then said Jesus again unto them, I go my way, and ye shall seek me, and **shall die in your sins**: whither I go, **ye cannot come**. (John 8:24)*

He tells them here that they will die in their sins and that they cannot come where he is going. That is some pretty straight language from the man who was generally so forgiving.

> *I speak that which I have seen with my Father: and ye do that which ye have seen with **your father**. They answered and said unto him, Abraham is our father. Jesus saith unto them, If ye were Abraham's children, ye would do the works of Abraham. But now ye seek to kill me, a man that hath told you the truth, which I have heard of God: this did not Abraham. Ye do the deeds of **your father**. Then said they to him, We be not born of fornication; we have one Father, even God. Jesus said unto them, If God were your Father, ye would love me: for I proceeded forth and came from God; neither came I of myself, but he sent me. Why do ye not understand my speech? even because **ye cannot hear my word. Ye are of your father the devil**, and the lusts of your father ye will do. He was a murderer from the beginning, and abode not in the truth, because there is no truth in him. When he speaketh a lie, he speaketh of his own: for he is a liar, and the father of it. And because I tell you the truth, ye believe me not. (John 8:38–45)*

Resurrection of the Unjust

Jesus did not pull any punches with them and did not even try to convert them because he knew that he could not. It was too late; they had made a commitment to the devil and had become his children, a reality that would have eternal ramifications.

Now let's look at the first quality associated with these "children of disobedience" to see if this all fits:

*And I saw thrones, and they sat upon them, and judgment was given unto them: and I saw the souls of them that were beheaded for the witness of Jesus, and for the word of God, and which **had not worshipped the beast, neither his image**, neither had received his mark upon their foreheads, or in their hands; and they lived and reigned with Christ a thousand years. (Revelation 20:4)*

Once again, if the participants of the first resurrection are those who have not worshiped the beast or his image, nor received the mark on their foreheads or in the hands, and the "rest of the dead" remain in the grave according to verse 5, then it stands to reason that the rest of the dead did worship the beast or his image and did receive the mark. Look at chapter 13:

*And they worshipped the dragon which gave power unto the beast: and **they worshipped the beast**,* *saying, Who is like unto the beast? who is able to make war with him? And there was given unto him a mouth speaking great things and* **blasphemies**; *and power was given unto him to continue forty and two months. And he opened his mouth in* **blasphemy against God, to blaspheme his name, and his tabernacle, and them that dwell in heaven.** *(Revelation 13:4–6)*

Notice the connection between the beast that is worshipped and blasphemy.

And deceiveth them that dwell on the earth by the means of those miracles which he had power to do in the sight of the beast; saying to them that dwell on the earth, that they should make an **image to the beast**, *which had the wound by a sword, and did live. And he had power to give life unto the* **image of the beast**, *that the* **image of the beast** *should both speak, and cause that as many as would not* **worship the image of the beast** *should be killed. And he causeth all, both small and great, rich and poor, free and bond, to* **receive a mark in their right hand, or in their foreheads:** *And that no man might buy or sell, save he that had the mark, or the name of the beast, or the number of his name. (Revelation 13:14–17)*

Resurrection of the Unjust

No doubt this will be a tough time to be alive. This is referring to the tribulation. But now we have the image of the beast being worshiped and the marks being associated. Revelation 14 has the same pattern:

> *And the third angel followed them, saying with a loud voice, If any man* **worship the beast and his image, and receive his mark in his forehead, or in his hand,** *The same shall drink of the wine of the wrath of God, which is poured out without mixture into the cup of his indignation; and he shall be tormented with fire and brimstone in the presence of the holy angels, and in the presence of the Lamb: And the smoke of their torment ascendeth up for ever and ever: and they have no rest day nor night,* **who worship the beast and his image, and whosoever receiveth the mark of his name.** *(Revelation 14:9–11)*

Notice how it states that "the same shall drink of the wine of the wrath of God," that they are going to be on the wrong side of that event when he comes to be with mankind. The same was said of the "children of disobedience" as we saw in Ephesians 5:6 and Colossians 3:6. Therefore, we can assert that they are one and the same.

> *And the first went, and poured out his vial upon the earth; and there fell a noisome and grievous sore upon the men which had the **mark of the beast, and upon them which worshipped his image**. (Revelation 16:2)*

These two ideas, worshipping his image and receiving the mark from Revelation 20:4, travel together through the record of the tribulation. Here we see the "wrath" coming upon them. Many believe that the Hebrew idiom of permission is employed in certain sections of the New Testament as well, and that would be the case here. In Revelation 19:20, the two are traveling together again, as well as the ultimate destiny of the beast and the false prophet:

> *And the beast was taken, and with him the false prophet that wrought miracles before him, with which he deceived them that had received **the mark of the beast**, and them that **worshipped his image**. These both were cast alive into a lake of fire burning with brimstone.*

We will reveal later exactly what is happening in this record, but for now, here is what we learned from these five sections of scripture in the book of Revelation:

- The connection between those who worshipped the beast and/or his image and those who received the mark
- How they will be on the wrong side of and excluded from the plans of God for the future
- The connection between all these things and blasphemy

Look at Revelation 2 now in the light of that understanding:

*I know thy works, and tribulation, and poverty, (but thou art rich) and I know the **blasphemy** of them which say they are Jews, and are not, but are the synagogue of Satan. (Revelation 2:9)*

A simple conclusion is that those who worship the beast and his image and receive the mark in their foreheads and hands are those who have blasphemed God and are of the synagogue of Satan. That doesn't take any spiritual discernment beyond reading what is written and tying verses together on the same subject.

That brings us to one of the main points of this study as we go back and look at what Jesus taught in Matthew 12:

> *Wherefore I say unto you, All manner of sin and blasphemy shall be forgiven unto men: but the blasphemy against the Holy Ghost shall not be forgiven unto men. And whosoever speaketh a word against the Son of man, it shall be forgiven him: but whosoever speaketh against the Holy Ghost, it shall not be forgiven him, neither in this world, neither in the world to come. (Matthew 12:31-32)*

Here we saw what has been referred to as "the unforgiveable sin." Notice that it is referred to as the "blasphemy against the Holy Ghost," which ties it into the references we examined in Revelation. These individuals will be part of the second resurrection: those who worshipped the beast and/or his image and who received the mark. Based on everything we have seen so far, it is not a matter of God's unwillingness to forgive but rather their unwillingness to repent, so they become eternal children of darkness. This does break God's heart, and although he has done and continues to do everything he can to dissuade that choice and commitment, he established free will as the first parameter back in the garden, and therefore he allows mankind that choice.

But what I want to draw your attention to is what is declared in this verse: "All manner of sin and blasphemy shall be forgiven unto men." That is not a simple future declaration, but it is an absolute. ALL MANNER OF SIN AND BLASPHEMY (with one exception) IS GOING TO BE FORGIVEN! Wouldn't that be wonderful? Doesn't that sound like the original message from the first century church of a loving, kind, and forgiving God? And knowing that Jesus is going to be the judge, and seeing his stance on forgiveness as displayed in John 8 and throughout the New Testament, this seems to fit. We are going to take the rest of this book to develop this idea to see if it stands.

The following questions no doubt arise at this point: When would this happen? When do those who die without making a commitment to either the True God or the devil receive this forgiveness? Is it a broad sweeping pardon passed upon all without repentance? No, this would not be fair to those who do confess and make Jesus lord. So when and how does this happen?

When speaking of the blasphemy against the Holy Ghost, Matthew 12:32 says it won't be forgiven either in this world or the world to come. Then it follows both logically and grammatically that all sin shall be forgiven either in this world or in the world to come. The word for "world" in the Greek text *aion* means "age." What our Lord and Savior was saying was that all sins are going to be forgiven either in this age or in the age to come. The millennial kingdom is when all deception will be removed while the devil, along with his entire kingdom will be sealed in the bottomless pit, and those who worshipped him will still be in the grave.

That gives Jesus Christ a full 1,000 years to preach his message of forgiveness and to reach those who did not confess and repent the first time around. Truly our God is the God of second chances, and they will have another opportunity to learn about him. They will actually get to see the Lord Jesus Christ face to face and see him for who he really is without lies or barriers. In that environment, God's only begotten Son, who came not into the world to condemn but to save it, will get the job done that his Father sent him to do:

> *Therefore judge nothing before the time, until the Lord come, who both will bring to light the hidden things of darkness, and will make manifest the counsels of the hearts: and then shall every man have praise of God. (1 Corinthians 4:5)*

> *That at the name of Jesus every knee should bow, of things in heaven, and things in earth, and things under the earth; And that every tongue should confess that Jesus Christ is Lord, to the glory of God the Father. (Philippians 2:10-11)*

9

God's Plan

THE BOOK OF Romans is the first epistle addressed to the church of our day and time. As such, it lays out many foundational doctrines and practical instructions to us. The section in chapters 9 through 11 is set apart grammatically and focuses on two main topics:

- The relationship and interaction between the Jews and the Gentiles
- The different dispensations or administrations that God divided history into that were governed by unique principles and guidelines, and more specifically, the Old Testament law and the New Testament grace periods

Regarding the second point, most everyone understands that we no longer need to sacrifice animals to gain forgiveness for sin. It is also generally understood that the Gospel is available to all in our day and time, not just one select nation of people. But did you ever wonder why God chose to divide history up into different periods and to focus on different groups of people the way he did?

This section sets for us one of the reasons he did it this way, and it ends with Paul's utter amazement and admiration of all God accomplished in so doing:

> *O the depth of the riches both of the wisdom and knowledge of God! how unsearchable are his judgments, and his ways past finding out! For who hath known the mind of the Lord? or who hath been his counsellor? Or who hath first given to him, and it shall be recompensed unto him again? For of him, and through him, and to him, are all things: to whom be glory for ever. Amen. (Romans 11:33-36)*

We will now begin to take a look at these chapters to see what Paul was so excited about:

> *I say the truth in Christ, I lie not, my conscience also bearing me witness in the Holy Ghost. (Romans 9:1)*

Paul opens this section with an emphatic declaration that what he is about to say is the truth:

- I say the truth in Christ
- I lie not

- My conscience also bearing witness in the Holy Ghost

He uses the figure of speech *repetitio*, communicating the same concept three different ways so the reader gets the point. The whole Word of God is true, so when this type of figure is used, it declares that what is coming is extremely important and may be hard for some to accept. As you will see, a key part of this message is that Israel is no longer the focus, and the Gentile nations are now in the spotlight. Can you imagine how that must have been received? The Israelites, the "chosen people of God" for thousands of years, including Paul himself, are now set aside, and they are no longer the only agents carrying out God's plan of redemption.

> *That I have great heaviness and continual sorrow in my heart. For I could wish that myself were accursed from Christ for my brethren, my kinsmen according to the flesh: Who are Israelites; to whom pertaineth the adoption, and the glory, and the covenants, and the giving of the law, and the service of God, and the promises; Whose are the fathers, and of whom as concerning the flesh Christ came, who is over all, God blessed for ever. Amen. (Romans 9:2–5)*

Here Paul is bearing his heart before the reader. He communicates how difficult this was for him and even says that he would be willing to surrender his salvation if it would change the outcome for them. He then gives them the "props" due from the Old Testament perspective. Yet the most interesting point in this section does not come through in the King James text. The figure of speech ***anamnesis***, meaning "reminiscence," is used in verse 3, and the word "could" should be understood as "used to."*

Paul used to feel the way he described in verses 2 and 3, but NOT ANYMORE. He is about to share with us in the next three chapters why he no longer feels that way. That ought to get our attention:

Not as though the word of God hath taken none effect. For they are not all Israel, which are of Israel. (Romans 9:6)

He starts verse 6 by saying it is "not as though the word of God hath taken none effect," or that it had failed. It might seem to be a failure, and that was what so burdened his heart. Israel's history was one of ups and downs. At the writing of this epistle, they were under Roman occupation. To add insult to injury, the long-awaited Messiah had finally come to them, and they rejected and killed him. It sure seems like a failure.

But now Paul knows differently. If there wasn't a second chance for them in the future, then Israel had their opportunity, blew it, and it's over for them. And if that were the case, then they died outside of God's will, and all they have to look forward to is judgment, when most believe they will be punished for their unbelief. But that is not the case, as Paul is about to reveal.

The first clue comes at the end of this verse: "They are not all Israel which are of Israel." While the majority of those God called did not stand, some of them did and changed the world in their day and time. The next ten verses show God's involvement in the process by calling those that he knew would stand (***the*** Israel of Israel):

> *Neither, because they are the seed of Abraham, are they all children: but, In Isaac shall thy seed be called. That is, They which are the children of the flesh, these are not the children of God: but the children of the promise are counted for the seed. For this is the word of promise, At this time will I come, and Sarah shall have a son. And not only this; but when Rebecca also had conceived by one, even by our father Isaac; (For the children being not yet born, neither having done any good or evil, that the purpose of God according to election might stand, not of works, but of him that calleth;) It was said unto her, The elder shall serve*

> *the younger. As it is written, Jacob have I loved, but Esau have I hated. What shall we say then? Is there unrighteousness with God? God forbid. For he saith to Moses, I will have mercy on whom I will have mercy, and I will have compassion on whom I will have compassion. So then it is not of him that willeth, nor of him that runneth, but of God that sheweth mercy. (Romans 9:7–16)*

A basic summary is that God worked through the individuals he called and helped them along by showing compassion and mercy. He had a plan that would include all of Israel in the end, and he achieved it without violating anyone's free will. By his foreknowledge, he called out certain ones he knew would rise to the occasion. The concept of his foreknowledge preceding his calling was handled in the immediately preceding context of chapter 8:

> *For whom he did **foreknow**, he also did **predestinate** to be conformed to the image of his Son, that he might be the firstborn among many brethren. Moreover whom he did **predestinate**, them he also **called**: and whom he called, them he also justified: and whom he justified, them he also glorified. (Romans 8:29–30)*

God's Plan

Romans 9:15-16 teaches us that God aided those he called by interjecting mercy into their lives, without which they would not have been able to bring his plan to pass. This extension of mercy was also introduced into the lives of his enemies, yet with them it produced a different reaction:

> *For the scripture saith unto Pharaoh, Even for this same purpose have I raised thee up, that I might shew my power in thee, and that my name might be declared throughout all the earth. Therefore hath he mercy on whom he will have mercy, and whom he will he hardeneth.* (Romans 9:17-18)

Verse 18 says that God hardened Pharaoh's heart, but the truth is, and always will be, that he does not violate free will. So what is being said here? This is another example of the "Hebrew idiom of permission" being employed where God is allowing the change in Pharaoh's heart to be attributed to him.

Verse 17 refers to the following scripture from the Old Testament:

> *And in very deed for this cause have I raised thee up, for to shew in thee my power; and that my name may be declared throughout all the earth.* (Exodus 9:16)

In this verse, the words "raised thee up" are better understood as "made thee to stand," or as translated in the Septuagint (the Greek rendering of the Old Testament), "preserved thee." We all know the record. There were a total of ten plagues that came against Egypt when Moses was demanding that Israel be set free. A closer look at this record in conjunction with a study of Egyptian culture reveals that these plagues were connected to the gods they worshipped. But every time Pharaoh repented and changed his mind, Moses came in and brought deliverance through the power of God.

These multiple acts of mercy had a different effect on Pharaoh, though, which is described in *The Companion Bible* this way:

> *It was in each case God's clemency and forbearing goodness which produced the hardening. That goodness which "leadeth to repentance" (Romans 2:4): just as the same sun which softens the wax hardens the clay.***

God knew in his foreknowledge that Pharaoh would not repent, no matter how much mercy was extended toward him. It is evident from this scenario and indicated by the context that Pharaoh was born of the seed of the serpent. So when God showed him mercy after mercy, it only emboldened him to continue in his opposition to God each time the consequences of his idolatry were removed. Therefore, it could be said that God hardened his heart simply by showing him mercy.

> *Thou wilt say then unto me, Why doth he yet find fault? For who hath resisted his will? Nay but, O man, who art thou that repliest against God? Shall the thing formed say to him that formed it, Why hast thou made me thus? Hath not the potter power over the clay, of the same lump to make one vessel unto honour, and another unto dishonour? (Romans 9:19–21)*

The next three verses communicate a human response to the situation. How can you blame Pharaoh for doing what you knew he would do? The answer is simply this: God knew in his foreknowledge that Pharaoh would sell out to the devil and become an eternal enemy, and there was nothing he could do to change that. (If the signs, wonders and miracles Pharaoh witnessed were not enough…) So knowing that, God chose to communicate a great truth in this situation by how he would interact with Pharaoh even AFTER he had already determined his destiny.

Then come two familiar verses that we have addressed several times, but in the context they shed even more light on the subject:

> *What if God, willing to shew his wrath, and to make his power known, endured with much longsuffering the vessels of wrath fitted to destruction: And that he might make known the riches of his glory on the vessels of mercy, which he had afore prepared unto glory. (Romans 9:22–23)*

Verse 22 then simply asks the question: What if all God was doing was displaying the extreme unconditionality of his great love (wrath) as well as the unrivaled greatness of his power toward a vessel of wrath fitted to destruction? God did not override his free will. Pharaoh had already made his choice, and God just used this situation as an opportunity to communicate the goodness of his nature toward all of mankind.

In the same manner, what if all of the mercy and compassion shown toward those he called from verses 7–16 was just a way for him to make known the riches of his glory? The truth is that God's intervention into the affairs of mankind did not supersede or overrule their free will choices, but instead, it unveiled truths in how he interacted with them in the context of their choices. And if that isn't enough, he was also fully engaged in bringing about his purpose for the ages. How brilliant is our God?

> *Even us, whom he hath called, not of the Jews only, but also of the Gentiles? As he saith also in Osee,*

God's Plan

I will call them my people, which were not my people; and her beloved, which was not beloved. And it shall come to pass, that in the place where it was said unto them, Ye are not my people; there shall they be called the children of the living God. Esaias also crieth concerning Israel, Though the number of the children of Israel be as the sand of the sea, a remnant shall be saved: For he will finish the work, and cut it short in righteousness: because a short work will the Lord make upon the earth. And as Esaias said before, Except the Lord of Sabaoth had left us a seed, we had been as Sodoma, and been made like unto Gomorrha. What shall we say then? That the Gentiles, which followed not after righteousness, have attained to righteousness, even the righteousness which is of faith. But Israel, which followed after the law of righteousness, hath not attained to the law of righteousness. Wherefore? Because they sought it not by faith, but as it were by the works of the law. For they stumbled at that stumblingstone; As it is written, Behold, I lay in Sion a stumblingstone and rock of offence: and whosoever believeth on him shall not be ashamed. (Romans 9:23–33)

In the context of "the vessels of mercy prepared unto glory," the Gentiles are now introduced, along with the documentation from the Old Testament that this was God's plan all along. He knew that only a few of his chosen people of Israel would get on board with what he was doing (the ISRAEL of Israel), so he devised his plan accordingly and shifted his focus to the Gentile nations.

God had given the law to Israel so that they would recognize the sin nature that was resident within them while at the same time setting parameters to contain it. The plan was for them to come to terms with the humbling reality that they would not be able to perfectly live up to the law's demands, and that they needed God's help. To the contrary, however, many were led to believe that the law was intended to be the avenue to attain righteousness, and as a result, they ended up either in condemnation or deception.

So what did God do? He introduced a new dispensation of time, referred to commonly as the "grace administration," where he gave righteousness to those who did only one thing: believe. They came to the humble recognition that they could not attain the righteousness of the law on their own. So they looked to God for help and accepted the gift of justification unto righteousness that he would bring through the accomplished work of his Son.

For many, as recorded in verse 33, this would become a stumbling block. But again, this did not take God by surprise. The next two chapters will lay out how this new "administration of grace" to the Gentile nations will demonstrate these truths and help them to overcome the obstacles that held them back the first time around. When they see the "uncircumcised" people from all the nations outside Israel who did not have the law clothed in the righteousness they sought all along, the lesson will finally hit home.

> *All of these had their merit attested because of their trusting. Nevertheless, they did not receive what had been promised, because God had planned something better that would involve us, so that only with us would they be brought to the goal. (Hebrews 11:39–40, Complete Jewish Bible)*

The Companion Bible, page 1680.
**The Companion Bible*, page 78.

10

Romans 10 and 11

THE 10TH CHAPTER of Romans is a significant section in the Word of God, building on the "stumbling block" that Jesus became to the hardhearted of Israel. In this chapter, an individual learns how to receive the salvation in Jesus Christ by confessing and believing alone. However, for the purposes of this study and for the sake of brevity, we are going to touch on only a few points within it.

The general gist of this chapter is how Jesus Christ would be the end of the law unto righteousness, how the proper understanding of the Old Testament revealed it, and how most of Israel missed that point. This message was made available through many different avenues so everyone had a chance to recognize its truth.

I know this may seem to be an oversimplification, but it is not my intention to make light of any part of God's Word. I desire to stay on track with this topic and focus only on those scriptures that contribute to it. What I would like to draw your attention to is the end of the chapter, where Paul introduces the Gentiles into the picture, and in particular verse 19, as this idea will come up again later:

> But I say, Did not Israel know? First Moses saith, I will **provoke you to jealousy** by them that are no people, and by a foolish nation I will anger you. (Romans 10:19)

God knew that the invitation to the Gentiles would not sit well with Israel. However, he once again chose a path that would ultimately be successful in converting their hearts, knowing how they would respond, and he worked his plan accordingly. This concept will be developed in the next chapter of Romans, and it will only make sense in the context of Israel being granted a second chance. If we believe that their opportunity to participate in what God was doing ended when they died, we will miss the greatness of what is revealed in this section.

> I say then, Hath God cast away his people? God forbid. For I also am an Israelite, of the seed of Abraham, of the tribe of Benjamin. (Romans 11:1)

Chapter 11 begins with a question that is likely to arise in the reader's mind. Paul himself shared this concern as reflected in the wording used at the beginning of chapter 9, but now he emphatically refutes the idea with "God forbid" and then points out that he himself is one of "his people." He now begins to explain why he no longer feels the way he did:

God hath not cast away his people which he foreknew. Wot ye not what the scripture saith of Elias? how he maketh intercession to God against Israel saying. (Romans 11:2)

He then counters the idea with a direct rebuttal: "God **hath not** cast away his people," *no matter what it might look like NOW.* He then refers to a similar situation from the Old Testament where it seemed as though things were not going according to God's plan at the time:

Lord, they have killed thy prophets, and digged down thine altars; and I am left alone, and they seek my life. But what saith the answer of God unto him? I have reserved to myself seven thousand men, who have not bowed the knee to the image of Baal. Even so then at this present time also there is a remnant according to the election of grace. (Romans 11:3–5)

Now, just like in the Old Testament, things are not always as they seem. God is an expert at bringing his will to pass, no matter what it looks like at the time. So often we look at things in terms of what the majority is doing, but God always has and will continue to work with the few.

*Not as though the word of God hath taken none effect. For they are not **all Israel, which are of Israel**. (Romans 9:6)*

There have always been true believers who do not sell out to the counterfeits of their day. Yet in any day and time, the few who move along with God's purposes are able to do so only because of special favor upon their lives. In the Old Testament, it was primarily mercy.

*So then it is not of him that willeth, nor of him that runneth, but of God that sheweth **mercy**. (Romans 9:16)*

In the New Testament, God draws our attention to the grace granted to those who are carrying out his will. The lesson that was missed by so many in the Old Testament is being taught by God's interaction with mankind in the New. Between both covenants, we have the full picture showing that without God's intervention in mercy and grace, mankind would fail miserably.

For us living during the time of the New Testament, we can learn about the mercy bestowed upon the Old

Testament believers by reading the recorded accounts. This gives us an unfair advantage over them since they did not have the benefit of seeing the part that grace would play in our lives. But God, who is perfectly just, has a plan whereby they will yet benefit from the things we are learning now, sometime in the future.

One lesson that grace taught us is succinctly stated in the next verse:

And if by grace, then is it no more of works: otherwise grace is no more grace. But if it be of works, then it is no more grace: otherwise work is no more work. (Romans 11:6)

This was the lesson that Israel needed to learn: The things God called them to do could not be accomplished by their works alone. They tried earning righteousness by way of their adherence to the law, but the truth was that no one could. For those who loved God and desired to serve him, he rewarded their efforts to live righteously with mercy when they failed. The New Testament took that concept a step further: In addition to the mercy for our missteps, there is also grace to take us beyond what we could accomplish on our own when we are walking in alignment with his will.

> *What then? Israel hath not obtained that which he seeketh for; but the election hath obtained it, and the rest were blinded. (Romans 11:7)*

There were those of Israel who did get it at the time and received the fruit thereof, and the Bible tracks them. This proves that if anyone figured it out, they all could have. The next verse is a quote from Isaiah elaborating on the blindness that came upon those who did not:

> *(According as it is written, God hath given them the spirit of slumber, eyes that they should not see, and ears that they should not hear;) unto this day. (Romans 11:8)*

After the Old Testament reference, by inspiration of God, Paul includes the words "unto this day," indicating that this blindness continues to the point of the writing of this epistle. However, this poses a question: Will this blindness continue beyond "this day"? If so, for how long? If it were to continue indefinitely, that phrase would serve no purpose. The answer to that question will be addressed later in this chapter.

Verses 9 and 10 are another quote from the Old Testament, and in particular the book of Psalms, regarding the blinded state of Israel. Then comes verse

11, which again poses a question that might come up as these truths are unveiled:

*I say then, Have they stumbled that they should fall? God forbid: but rather through their fall salvation is come unto the Gentiles, **for to provoke them to jealousy**. (Romans 11:11)*

Was it God's plan for Israel to fail? Once again, the phrase is used and the answer is a very emphatic: "God forbid." It is never God's will that mankind fail, even though we will many times. God in his omniscient compassion crafted a plan once again, using the human response of those outside his will to redirect them back to it. God is a master at doing this, and the Bible is the story of this perfect work in its fullness.

So what was God's plan? He set up a new administration whereby salvation would be obtained by grace alone, and then he made it available to the rest of the world, knowing that this would provoke Israel to jealousy and establish that truth he had communicated in chapter 10:

*But I say, Did not Israel know? First Moses saith, I will **provoke you to jealousy** by them that are no people, and by a foolish nation I will anger you. (Romans 10:19)*

The quote of Moses from Deuteronomy chapter 32 reveals that God had this plan all along. Somehow the jealousy that would result in his grace toward the Gentiles, and even the anger that would be birthed from it, would contribute to their learning the lesson they missed the first time around.

> *Now if the fall of them be the riches of the world, and the diminishing of them the riches of the Gentiles; how much more their fulness? (Romans 11:12)*

If the stumbling of Israel brought about such a positive impact to the rest of the world, just imagine what their walking in accordance with it will bring. (Spoiler alert.)

> *For I speak to you Gentiles, inasmuch as I am the apostle of the Gentiles, I magnify mine office: If by any means I may* **provoke to emulation** *them which are my flesh, and might save some of them. (Romans 11:13-14)*

Here, God's plan is set forth a third time so there is no missing it. The word here for "emulation" is the exact same one used as "jealousy" in Romans 10:19 and 11:11. There can be no question about it—this was the plan.

A casual reading of the Gospels, the book of Acts, and the epistles shows that it was successful. Once again, the question is the timeframe involved. Here in verse 14, the reference is to Paul's attempt to save some of Israel in his lifetime, and that it was God's calling for him as an Israelite. Hold that thought and let's continue.

> *For if the casting away of them be the reconciling of the world, what shall the receiving of them be, but life from the dead? (Romans 11:15)*

Once again, if the rejection of Israel brought reconciliation to the world, what will it be like when they are back in his will?

> *For if the firstfruit be holy, the lump is also holy: and if the root be holy, so are the branches. And if some of the branches be broken off, and thou, being a wild olive tree, wert grafted in among them, and with them partakest of the root and fatness of the olive tree; Boast not against the branches. But if thou boast, thou bearest not the root, but the root thee. Thou wilt say then, The branches were broken off, that I might be grafted in. Well; because of unbelief they were broken off, and thou standest by faith. Be not highminded, but fear: For if God spared not the natural branches, take heed lest he*

> *also spare not thee. Behold therefore the goodness and severity of God: on them which fell, severity; but toward thee, goodness, if thou continue in his goodness: otherwise thou also shalt be cut off. And they also, if they abide not still in unbelief, shall be grafted in: for God is able to graft them in again. For if thou wert cut out of the olive tree which is wild by nature, and wert grafted contrary to nature into a good olive tree: how much more shall these, which be the natural branches, be grafted into their own olive tree? (Romans 11:16–24)*

This section of scripture was to provide a perspective for the reader. Here the Gentiles are instructed to remain humble and to recognize that it was mainly God's doing for them to be part of his plan, and that their inclusion was a result of believing alone, so unbelief could affect them as well. They are also reminded that the children of Israel were the original people chosen, and that God found a way to include the Gentiles into the plan and not vice versa.

Notice that in verse 23, it records that Israel could be grafted back in if they "abide not still in unbelief." Is this a temporal thing only, and does the chance for them end when they are deceased? The next section of scripture will answer that question:

Romans 10 and 11

For I would not, brethren, that ye should be ignorant of this mystery, lest ye should be wise in your own conceits; that blindness in part is happened to Israel, until the fulness of the Gentiles be come in. (Romans 11:25)

This is a very critical and pivotal verse to understand. God is ready to unveil another mystery or "secret" that will help the Gentiles keep the proper perspective and not get influenced by pride. The blindness regarding Israel spoken of throughout this section will end at a certain point: "The fullness of the Gentiles." So now the question becomes, when does this take place?

What if the very last words spoken by Jesus Christ before he ascended into heaven gave us the answer?

But ye shall receive power, after that the Holy Ghost is come upon you: and ye shall be witnesses unto me both in Jerusalem, and in all Judaea, and in Samaria, and unto the uttermost part of the earth. (Acts 1:8)

Jesus instructed his followers to be his witnesses with power starting in Jerusalem and then in all Judea, reaching out to their fellow countrymen. From that point they would move on to Samaria to those who were considered "half-Jews," moving in the direction of the

Gentile nations. Their final goal was the uttermost part of the earth, which would certainly include them. Could the "uttermost part of the earth" be the same thing as "the fulness of the Gentiles," a journey begun in the book of Acts and yet to be completed? And could it be that the fulfillment of this assignment, given by the Lord Jesus Christ on his ascension to heaven, is what is necessary to trigger his return?

Now take a look at what comes next in the 11th chapter of Romans:

> **And so all Israel shall be saved:** *as it is written, There shall come out of Sion the Deliverer, and shall turn away ungodliness from Jacob. (Romans 11:26)*

Did you catch that? Could it really be true, that God in his infinite wisdom, grace, mercy, and love figured out a way to save all of Israel without overstepping their free will? This would be the perfect fulfillment of many Old Testament records, summed up here in the quotes from Isaiah at the end of this verse and in verse 27:

> *As it is written, There shall come out of Sion the Deliverer, and shall turn away ungodliness from Jacob: For this is my covenant unto them, when I shall take away their sins. (Romans 11:26-27)*

Verse 27 is a combination of scriptures from Isaiah that Paul by revelation linked together. It is worded in such a way that is extremely intriguing: that taking away the sins of Israel was God's covenant or promise unto them. God never fails on his promises. In this context, look again at what is recorded of Jesus in Matthew chapter 12:

*Wherefore I say unto you, **All manner of sin and blasphemy shall be forgiven unto men**: but the blasphemy against the Holy Ghost shall not be forgiven unto men. (Matthew 12:31)*

Is it possible that God's plan to save Israel through his Son Jesus Christ will ultimately be a lot more successful than we may have realized? Just imagine the Lord moving about during the first resurrection, his millennial kingdom, where everyone who rejected him the first time around would have an opportunity to see him clearly for who he really is. The partial blindness would be removed with all the deceivers either still in the pit (Satan and his kingdom) or in the grave (those who worshipped the beast and received the mark), and he would have a thousand years in that setting to penetrate their unbelief. If all those things are true, how hard would it be to imagine that the Lord Jesus Christ could achieve a success rate of 100 percent in his second attempt to win Israel?

The way that this narrative comes full circle in such a perfect way is beautiful. Back in Romans 9:6, as Paul began to communicate the new understanding of how the Old Testament was not a failure, he wrote, "They are not all Israel which are of Israel." Here toward the end of this section of scripture, he ends by saying, "And so all Israel shall be saved." Putting those two ideas side by side: "They are not all Israel which are of Israel," but in the end, "All Israel shall be saved." Even though not everyone God called participated in his plan, in the end all of them will benefit. Isn't that the story of the Bible, how the many are saved by the few? And ultimately how all are saved by one: the Lord Jesus Christ, the stumbling block. This was something Paul was very excited about, and we should be, too.

As concerning the gospel, they are enemies for your sakes: but as touching the election, they are beloved for the father's sakes. For the gifts and calling of God are without repentance. (Romans 11:28–29)

At the time of the writing of this epistle, Israel was being provoked to jealousy as Moses foretold, becoming an enemy to the movement of the Gospel. Nonetheless, the calling of God is without repentance: he called them, he still loves them, he does not change his mind, and he is not through with them yet. In the future, the stage will be set and they will get a second chance and make the right decision at that time.

> *For as ye in times past have not believed God, yet have now obtained mercy through their unbelief: Even so have these also now not believed, that through your mercy they also may obtain mercy. For God hath concluded them all in unbelief, that he might have mercy upon all. (Romans 11:30-32)*

For now, therefore, mercy should be extended toward Israel. The Gentile nations were the unbelievers in the past and were the enemies of God's plan concerning Israel as a result. Now that things have turned around, it is time that the Gentiles extend to Israel the same mercy that they have received, for in the end, all of mankind deals with unbelief. Throughout the history of the world and the different administrations God has divided it into, all of humanity is learning on a cumulative basis. A future dispensation is coming whereby everyone who missed the lesson along the way will get a chance to see it in its entirety. What a beautiful plan and one worthy of great admiration and praise:

> *Have you ever come on anything quite like this extravagant generosity of God, this deep, deep*

wisdom? It's way over our heads. We'll never figure it out.

Is there anyone around who can explain God?
Anyone smart enough to tell him what to do?
Anyone who has done him such a huge favor
 that God has to ask his advice?
Everything comes from him;
Everything happens through him;
Everything ends up in him.
Always glory! Always praise!
 Yes. Yes. Yes.
(Romans 11:33–36 The Message)

11

Weeping and Gnashing of Teeth

OUR STUDY OF Romans 9 through 11 taught us that God is not done with Israel, and that they were not a failure in the Old Testament, regardless of what it appeared to be. He had a plan that was being worked by the few that would in the end save them all. The next step in his plan was the introduction of the grace administration, where the things that the Old Testament believers endeavored to earn would be given away freely to all the nations through the accomplishment of one: the Lord Jesus Christ.

This is still a plan in progress, which will be finalized at some point in the future. Jesus taught many things about his future millennial kingdom, and in these teachings we will see the truths from Romans lived out.

It is interesting to me that the records we will be examining are the same that many Bible scholars have used to build their case for an angry God and the hellfire and brimstone concept. I am talking about the records in the Gospels regarding "weeping and gnashing of teeth." We are going to study the seven different accounts where

Jesus taught about this and add to what we've built so far. The truth conveyed is actually much different from what immediately comes to mind.

As we look at these records, please keep in mind the following questions:

- Who is involved?
- Where do those involved end up?
- When does the record take place?

We will start with the first record in Matthew chapter 8:

But the children of the kingdom shall be cast out into outer darkness: there shall be weeping and gnashing of teeth. (Matthew 8:12)

This particular record was used in something I once read as an example of Jesus' teachings about hell. It is interesting to note that the word "hell" does not appear. Let's answer our three questions:

- Who is involved? The answer is very clear: the children of the kingdom.
- Where do those involved end up? Again the answer is clear: outer darkness.

Weeping and Gnashing of Teeth

- When does this record take place? The prior verse contains the answer:

*And I say unto you, That many shall come from the east and west, and shall sit down with Abraham, and Isaac, and Jacob, **in the kingdom of heaven**. (Matthew 8:11)*

This event Jesus was teaching about will take place in the kingdom of heaven. The tense of the verbs "shall come" and "shall sit down" indicate that this is an event in the future and specifically the millenial kingdom. The greater context is the healing of the servant of a centurion who was a soldier in the Roman army and therefore not one of the children of Israel. His servant was extremely ill and at the point of death. The centurion came to Jesus asking him to heal his servant, and Jesus offered to go to his home with him. The centurion understood both how this would be a violation of Jewish law and how authority worked, and therefore he trusted that Jesus could just speak the healing right then and there and it would happen.

When Jesus heard it, he marvelled, and said to them that followed, Verily I say unto you, I have not found so great faith, no, not in Israel. (Matthew 8:10)

This blew Jesus mind! Can you imagine that? This is the only time that anyone caused Jesus to marvel in a positive sense, and the man was a Gentile. Jesus took this opportunity to teach a truth regarding the future. During his millennial kingdom, many will come from "the uttermost part of the earth" and join him with some of the great believers of Israel. Some believe that he referred to them indirectly, as from "the east and west" instead of "the Gentiles," so as to avoid offending them so early in his ministry and provoking them to jealousy.

But many of the children of the kingdom, those from the Old Testament understood to be the chosen of God, would not gain entrance to that gathering, but instead they would be cast out into "outer darkness." What exactly does that mean? Notice it doesn't say hell, and there's no indication of fire or brimstone. This phrase is used only three times in the Bible, and all three times are in the context of weeping and gnashing of teeth.

The word "outer" means the outermost or most remote, and the word for "darkness" refers to the absence of light. In *The Companion Bible*, Bullinger describes this place as simply "outside the place where the feast was going on in verse 11."*

Please note also that there is no reference to the time involved. Nor is there any indication that this will be their final destination for all eternity. These are all simple truths that are clearly seen by reading the section. Let's move on to the next occurrence:

And shall cast them into a furnace of fire: there shall be wailing and gnashing of teeth. (Matthew 13:42)

In this second usage, the word "wailing" is used instead of "weeping," but it is the exact same word in the original Greek texts. Let's answer our three questions regarding this record:

- Who is involved? The prior verse gives us the answer:

The Son of man shall send forth his angels, and they shall gather out of his kingdom all things that offend, **and them which do iniquity.** *(Matthew 13:41)*

It is all things that offend, or all offences, and **them which do iniquity.** This word for "iniquity" is another key in our study. It is *anomia* in the Greek, which means "lawlessness." It goes beyond the occasional sin here and there to the level of a complete disregard for the law. This word and concept will come up again many times in future chapters of this book.

So who are the lawless? The previously explained parable lays it out as plain as day. Jesus first communicated it this way:

> *Another parable put he forth unto them, saying, The kingdom of heaven is likened unto a man which sowed good seed in his field: But while men slept, his enemy came and sowed tares among the wheat, and went his way. But when the blade was sprung up, and brought forth fruit, then appeared the tares also. So the servants of the householder came and said unto him, Sir, didst not thou sow good seed in thy field? from whence then hath it tares? He said unto them, An enemy hath done this. The servants said unto him, Wilt thou then that we go and gather them up? But he said, Nay; lest while ye gather up the tares, ye root up also the wheat with them. Let both grow together until the harvest: and in the time of harvest I will say to the reapers, Gather ye together first* **the tares, and bind them in bundles to burn them**: *but gather the wheat into my barn. (Matthew 13:24–30)*

In this illustration, it is the tares that get burned, and yet who they represent is not clear. When Jesus finished this parable, he went right into two others that had similar themes. They both communicated that the kingdom of God might not look like much right now, but in the future it will grow significantly. It kind of reminds me of one the main lessons learned in Romans 9–11, that God will ultimately save the many by way of the few.

> *Another parable put he forth unto them, saying, The kingdom of heaven is like to a grain of mustard seed, which a man took, and sowed in his field: Which indeed is the least of all seeds: but when it is grown, it is the greatest among herbs, and becometh a tree, so that the birds of the air come and lodge in the branches thereof. Another parable spake he unto them; The kingdom of heaven is like unto leaven, which a woman took, and hid in three measures of meal, till the whole was leavened. (Matthew 13:31–33)*

Later in what appears to be the same day, the disciples came to Jesus and asked him to clarify what he was communicating with the parable of the tares:

> *Then Jesus sent the multitude away, and went into the house: and his disciples came unto him, saying, Declare unto us the parable of the tares of the field. (Matthew 13:36)*

The word "declare" means to "explain" or "interpret." In one of the Greek texts, it is translated "make quite plain." I find this very intriguing, because Jesus does just exactly that. In his response, he makes it simple and clear, defining each and every term. I believe he will do the same thing today if we ask the same thing of him.

> *He answered and said unto them, He that soweth the good seed is the Son of man; The field is the world; the good seed are the children of the kingdom; but the **tares are the children of the wicked one**; The enemy that sowed them is the devil; the harvest is the end of the world; and the reapers are the angels. As therefore the tares are gathered and burned in the fire; so shall it be in the end of this world. (Matthew 13:37–40)*

The tares are the children of the wicked one. Now we know the "who" of this second occurrence. It is very clear and needs no guesswork. Notice that there are only two categories of children: those of the kingdom and those of the wicked one. In his parable about the end times, he doesn't include a third group of the unsaved. The question should arise as to why not? Could it be that there will be only two groups at the end of time? Hold that thought.

Now we look at the other two questions:

Weeping and Gnashing of Teeth

- Where do those involved end up? We see a different destination for this group, and if we include both parables as well as the statement in verse 42, it is "burned in a furnace of fire."
- When does this event take place? The clearest description is in the unveiling of the parable to the disciples in verse 40: the end of this world. Once again, the word for world is *aion*, which is best translated "age."

So after the first two occurrences of weeping and gnashing, we have learned that they regard two different groups of people with two different destinations, happening at two different times. The children of the kingdom end up in outer darkness during the kingdom, but the children of the wicked one end up in a furnace of fire at the end of the age. Now the question is this: Will these distinctions continue on through the rest of the five occurrences? Before we look at the next record, I would like to draw your attention to the truth communicated in the very next verse:

Then shall the righteous shine forth as the sun in the kingdom of their Father. Who hath ears to hear, let him hear. (Matthew 13:43)

The same event that will cause the children of the wicked one to be burned in a furnace of fire will cause the righteous to "shine forth as the sun." This will make complete sense by the time the book is over.

The next occurrence appears just six verses later:

So shall it be at the end of the world: the angels shall come forth, and sever the wicked from among the just, And shall cast them into the furnace of fire: there shall be wailing and gnashing of teeth. (Matthew 13:49–50)

Now let's look at the three questions regarding this occurrence to see if the pattern repeats itself:

- Who is involved? Here in verse 49, it is the "wicked." This is the same word used in verse 38 in the phrase "wicked one." Could it be that the children of the wicked one are themselves wicked, just as the children of God take on his nature?
- Where do those involved end up? These end up in the furnace of fire.
- When does the record take place? At the end of the "world," again more properly translated "age."

Weeping and Gnashing of Teeth

So let's look at this. This occurrence refers to the wicked, and they end up in a furnace of fire at the end of the age. This fits perfectly with the second occurrence, and if the wicked are indeed the tares, then they are the children of the wicked one.

The next occurrence appears in chapter 22 of Matthew:

> *Then said the king to the servants, Bind him hand and foot, and take him away, and cast him into outer darkness, there shall be weeping and gnashing of teeth. (Matthew 22:13)*

In this account, we have to do a little more digging to get the answers to our three questions. Right off the bat, we can see that the destination for this individual is outer darkness. That is clear from the verse itself. But to find out who is involved and when this takes place, we have to dig a little deeper. Matthew 22:2 gives us the answer as to when this record takes place:

> *The **kingdom of heaven** is like unto a certain king, which made a marriage for his son.*

This is a parable regarding the kingdom of heaven, and not the end of the age. So far, that fits with the first occurrence we examined about the children of the kingdom. The "who" is found in the two previous verses:

And when the king came in to see the guests, he saw there a man which had not on a wedding garment: And he saith unto him, Friend, how camest thou in hither not having a wedding garment? And he was speechless. (Matthew 22:11–12)

The individual was a wedding guest who did not properly dress for the event. Jesus then addresses him as "friend." This word can be defined as a companion, associate, partner, or comrade. This is not an enemy in any way. Since this event takes place during the kingdom, and the destination is outer darkness, then these terms would be additional descriptions of a "child of the kingdom." However, the point Jesus is making is that the person showed up without preparing properly for the wedding, so he was not allowed to participate. The greater truth is that he was not yet "clothed in righteousness," so he still had to confess and repent.

As we will see in the final three occurrences, the pattern continues with additional insights provided through the descriptions of the individuals involved or their final destination.

The next verse is very intriguing. At first glance, it appears to be a contradiction to what we are setting forth so far. This will require a chapter of its own, and we will address it after this study.

For many are called, but few are chosen. (Matthew 22:14)

**The Companion Bible*, page 1324.

12

Weeping and Gnashing Continued

IN THE FIRST four occurrences of weeping and gnashing of teeth, a pattern has been set. We have looked at three components of these events to develop that pattern: who, where, and when. What we have seen so far is that during the millennial kingdom, some of the children destined for the kingdom will not partake in its festivities from the start. Instead, they will spend some time outside as they work through their confession of and repentance from sin.

We have also seen a second group of people—the children of the enemy who will end up in a furnace of fire at the end of the age. In the remaining three occurrences of weeping and gnashing of teeth, the focus will be on the first group only. Neither the enemies of God nor the furnace of fire will come up again.

Jesus taught about the children of the kingdom and what will happen to them on numerous occasions. We will see in the remaining three occurrences how he added insights and instructions by the different ways he described one or more of the components we are examining. Bearing this in mind, let's look at the fifth occurrence in Matthew chapter 24:

And shall cut him asunder, and appoint him his portion with the hypocrites: there shall be weeping and gnashing of teeth. (Matthew 24:51)

This last verse in Matthew 24 does not tell us who it is referring to. We will have to look at the prior context to determine who it is talking about when it says "him":

*But and if that **evil servant** shall say in his heart, My lord delayeth his coming; And shall begin to smite his fellowservants, and to eat and drink with the drunken; The lord of that servant shall come in a day when he looketh not for him, and in an hour that he is not aware of. (Matthew 24:48–50)*

Here we see in verse 48 that is speaking of a servant who is evil. The three verses before that refer to a faithful and wise servant:

*Who then is a **faithful and wise servant**, whom his lord hath made ruler over his household, to give them meat in due season? Blessed is that servant, whom his lord when he cometh shall find*

Weeping and Gnashing Continued

so doing. Verily I say unto you, That he shall make him ruler over all his goods. (Matthew 24:45–47)

The overall context in the nine verses before that is the timing of the Lord's coming, and how no one knows when that will be. All of this background is necessary in understanding who this fifth occurrence of weeping and gnashing of teeth is referring to. Jesus first teaches about the faithful and wise servant, who is busy with the responsibility given him when the Lord returns and the rewards that he will receive as a result.

In contrast, the evil servant is the one who believes that the Lord's coming will be delayed, and so he abdicates his responsibility, is surprised when he does show up unexpectedly, and is not prepared for the consequences. Much is to be learned by comparing and contrasting the two, but now we know who this is referring to: an ill-prepared servant of the Lord and therefore another "child of the kingdom."

In searching for the subject of this occurrence, we have also learned when it happened: at the coming of the Lord. In contrast, you may recall that the children of the evil one will end up in the furnace of fire *at the end* of the age.

So now we will discover where this evil servant will end up. If the pattern we have established so far continues, then this place will be equivalent to "outer darkness." That answer is found directly in the verse we are focusing on:

> *And shall cut him **asunder, and appoint him his portion with the hypocrites**: there shall be weeping and gnashing of teeth. (Matthew 24:51)*

The word "asunder" is very intriguing. It is translated from the Greek word *dichotomeo*, which literally means to cut into two parts. *Vine's Expository Dictionary of New Testament Words* adds the following insight:

> *Some take the reference to be to the mode of punishment by which criminals and captives were cut in two; others, on account of the fact that in [this] passage the delinquent is still surviving after the treatment, take the verb to denote to cut up by scourging, to scourge severely, the word being used figuratively.**

Whether figurative or literal, the evil servant receives punishing consequences for his behavior upon the return of his lord. Instead of enjoying the presence of his lord with the faithful and wise servants, he instead spends his time with the hypocrites. Again, notice that there is no mention of this condition being permanent.

Weeping and Gnashing Continued

Two interesting translations of Matthew 24:51 are as follows:

That servant will then be punished and thrown out with the ones who only pretended to serve their master. There they will cry and grit their teeth in pain. (Contemporary English Version)

He'll end up in the dump with the hypocrites, out in the cold shivering, teeth chattering. (The Message)

The next occurrence is found in the following chapter:

And cast ye the unprofitable servant into outer darkness: there shall be weeping and gnashing of teeth. (Matthew 25:30)

In this occurrence, the "who" and the "where" are found in the verse: it is referring to the "unprofitable servant" who ends up in "outer darkness." So in looking at the usage before, we can draw the conclusion that outer darkness, a place outside of the marriage feast, is not just for the evil servants but for the unprofitable servant as well. So much can be learned by studying the context and the topic of unprofitability, which no doubt was our Lord's intention.

To discover when this takes place, one needs to go all the way up to verse 14, which is the beginning of the parable that ends in verse 30:

> *For the kingdom of heaven is as a man travelling into a far country, who called his own servants, and delivered unto them his goods. (Matthew 25:14)*

When looking at this scripture in the King James Version, the words "the kingdom of heaven is as" are italicized, indicating that they were not in the original text but added by the translators. The first word, "For," ties it to the previous verse, explaining why that assumption was made:

> *Watch therefore, for ye know neither the day nor the hour wherein the Son of man cometh. (Matthew 25:13)*

Verse 19 specifically clarifies the timing of this event:

> *After a long time the lord of those servants cometh, and reckoneth with them. (Matthew 25:19)*

Weeping and Gnashing Continued

Again, as with the last occurrence, the timing of this event is linked to the return of the lord, which is unknown to the servant. The difference this time is that the servant is merely unprofitable, in the sense that nothing has been done with the resources made available by the lord in his absence.

Putting this all together, we can deduce that the unprofitable servant will also miss out on the festivities available when the lord returns. Once again, I draw your attention to the fact that there is no indication that this is a permanent situation.

The seventh and final occurrence of weeping and gnashing of teeth is found in the book of Luke:

There shall be weeping and gnashing of teeth, when ye shall see Abraham, and Isaac, and Jacob, and all the prophets, **in the kingdom of God,** *and you yourselves thrust out. (Luke 13:28)*

In this usage, it is pretty easy to determine when it takes place: "In the kingdom of God." These individuals are to be thrust outside the place where Abraham, Isaac, Jacob, and all the prophets are, which fits with our original interpretation of "outer darkness."

To determine who this record is speaking about, we need to do a little more digging. It is obvious that the individuals being spoken to are the subject of this verse:

"You yourselves." The prior verse provides additional insight into this group:

But he shall say, I tell you, I know you not whence ye are; depart from me, all ye workers of iniquity. (Luke 13:27)

Here, the word for iniquity means "unrighteousness," or simply that which does not conform to what is right. "Workers of iniquity" do things contrary to what is right and true. Many fall into this category, yet once again, there is no indication whatsoever that it is a permanent reality.

In summation, what have we learned regarding the seven occurrences of weeping and gnashing of teeth?

One point that should be clear, contrary to a widely held opinion that these records describe hell, is that only two of the seven end up in a furnace of fire. In both cases, this takes place at the end of the age, and it is clearly a place destined only for the lawless or the children of the wicked one.

The rest of the occurrences focus on the children of the kingdom, and they take place either at the very beginning when the Lord returns or sometime before the end of that age. In all of these occurrences, those involved are denied entry to the events taking place with the Lord during his kingdom. In these five occurrences, much is

Weeping and Gnashing Continued

to be learned in the different descriptions of the three components we viewed. It makes sense that the Lord would focus most of his instruction on those who will be part of that kingdom, teaching them what to avoid in this life and how to participate in what is coming in the next.

The dichotomy that began in Genesis 3 continues into the teachings of the Lord Jesus Christ. In the end, there will be only two groups of people with two ultimate destinies. One group, comprising those who choose to align themselves with darkness or the "seed of the serpent," is destroyed at the end of the age. Everyone else, however, will make it into the coming kingdom, although there is an order to when they will enter. Some will experience hardship in the process, and will not gain access from the very beginning. The point that is starting to emerge is that everyone but the "seed of the serpent" will make it into the kingdom by the end of the age.

Vine's Expository Dictionary of New Testament Words, page 266.

13

Many Are Called but Few Chosen

THE FIRST TIME I worked through the usages of "weeping and gnashing of teeth," I came upon the following verse after the fourth occurrence, and it stopped me in my tracks:

> *Then said the king to the servants, Bind him hand and foot, and take him away, and cast him into outer darkness, there shall be weeping and gnashing of teeth.* ***For many are called, but few are chosen.*** *(Matthew 22:13-14)*

If many are called but only a few are chosen, then it appears that the outcome of Jesus' work will not be quite as successful as I had thought. Or could it just be that I don't really understand what he was saying when he made that statement.

When I began to look at that phrase, I discovered that it occurred previously, just a couple of chapters before:

*So the last shall be first, and the first last: **for many be called, but few chosen**. (Matthew 20:16)*

This time, the truth is linked to another one that seems to add additional light to the subject. The idea of "many [being] called, but few chosen" is grammatically connected to "so the last shall be first, and the first last." Now I am really confused. And if that is not enough, the statement at the beginning of Matthew 20:16 occurs one other time as well, just one chapter earlier, where it is worded slightly differently and in a reverse order:

But many that are first shall be last; and the last shall be first. (Matthew 19:30)

So there you have it: two truths linked together grammatically and logically and all tied into the fourth occurrence of "weeping and gnashing of teeth." Let's begin to unpack all of this, to see what we can learn from what Jesus was teaching in these four chapters from the gospel of Matthew and what they tell us about the parable of weeping and gnashing of teeth in chapter 22.

We will start with the second occurrence in Matthew 22 of "many called but few chosen." I would like to draw your attention to the word at the beginning of the phrase—a little word with a big meaning:

Many Are Called but Few Chosen

For many are called, but few are chosen. (Matthew 22:14)

The word "for" at the beginning of this phrase is a contraction of two words in the Greek: "verily" and "therefore."* It is another way of saying the same thing, but more concisely. The Good News Translation renders Matthew 22:13–14 this way:

"Then the king told the servants, 'Tie him up hand and foot, and throw him outside in the dark. There he will cry and gnash his teeth.'" **And Jesus concluded,** *"Many are invited, but few are chosen."*

Therefore, if we can understand what Jesus meant by the phrase "many be called, but few chosen," we can have some additional insight to this record of weeping and gnashing of teeth. It is interesting to note that the previous usage also begins with the word "for," and it is the exact same contraction in the Greek:

So the last shall be first, and the first last: ***for*** *many be called, but few chosen. (Matthew 20:16)*

In like manner, if we can understand what Jesus meant by "the last being first and the first last," we can have a better understanding of "many are called but few chosen." Both of these phrases will shed additional light on the occurrence of weeping and gnashing of teeth. Are you with me so far?

Let's start back in Matthew 19:30 with the first occurrence of these three scriptures and work our way forward.

> **But** many that are first shall be last; and the last shall be first. (Matthew 19:30)

Notice the first word in this phrase: "but." It is another one of those little words with a big meaning. This connects two ideas by contrasting them. If we look at the context in the section before it, we can better understand the truth Jesus was conveying.

The account is about a rich man who asked Jesus what he needed to do to inherit eternal life:

> And someone came to Him and said, "Teacher, what [essentially] good thing shall I do to obtain eternal life [that is, **eternal salvation in the Messiah's kingdom**]?" (Matthew 19:16 Amplified Bible)

He wanted to know how he would be able to enter the kingdom and live forever. In the end, Jesus told him to sell his possessions and follow him. The young man

Many Are Called but Few Chosen

was not ready to make that level of commitment, and Jesus made the following observation:

Then said Jesus unto his disciples, Verily I say unto you, That a rich man shall hardly enter into the kingdom of heaven. (Matthew 19:23)

The King James Version seems to support the idea that not many will be saved. However, the word for "hardly" in the original text doesn't mean "scarcely, or to an insignificant degree" as the word might communicate to us, but it actually means more along the lines of "with hardship."

The Darby Translation of the verse puts it this way:

*And Jesus said to his disciples, Verily I say unto you, A rich man **shall with difficulty** enter into the kingdom of the heavens. (Matthew 19:23)*

That is a different statement altogether. The rich man may eventually enter into the kingdom of God, but it just won't be easy for him. The next verse also communicates the difficulty through which most rich men will enter into the kingdom:

And again I say unto you, It is easier for a camel to go through the eye of a needle, than for a rich man to enter into the kingdom of God. (Matthew 19:24)

The disciples were shocked by this statement and asked a pointed question. Look closely at Jesus' response:

When his disciples heard it, they were exceedingly amazed, saying, Who then can be saved? But Jesus beheld them, and said unto them, With men this is impossible; **but with God all things are possible**. *(Matthew 19:25–26)*

Even though it may be difficult for some to enter, God has made a way. This is a lesson for all: On our own, it is impossible for us to enter the kingdom of God. Without God's grace and mercy, none of us would stand a chance. ***But***—and that's emphatic—**with God all things are possible**.

Desiring to avoid a similar fate, Peter asks a question. Jesus responds and teaches the disciples what they can do now to prepare for entrance into the kingdom:

Then answered Peter and said unto him, Behold, we have forsaken all, and followed thee; what shall we have therefore? And Jesus said unto them, Verily I say unto you, That ye which have followed me, in the regeneration when the Son of man shall sit in the throne of his glory, ye also shall sit upon twelve thrones, judging the twelve tribes of Israel. And every one that hath forsaken houses, or brethren, or sisters, or father, or mother, or wife, or children, or lands, for my name's sake, shall receive an hundredfold, and shall inherit everlasting life. (Matthew 19:27-29)

Simply put, those who prepare for eternity by prioritizing it above the things of this world will gain entrance into the kingdom and reap the rewards for their efforts.

And then comes our verse:

But many that are first shall be last; and the last shall be first. (Matthew 19:30)

A simple cursory reading of this verse communicates the following. If you have two groups, the "first" and the "last," and they are both heading somewhere but one group arrives there "last" and the other "first," what do you know about both groups? **They both get there; it is only a matter of when they get there, not whether or not they both make it.** Let's put it another way. I have Group A and Group B leaving St. Louis and heading to Chicago. If Group A is *first* to arrive and group B is *last*, what do we know about both A and B? They both make it to Chicago, or in this case *"eternal salvation in the Messiah's kingdom."*

In contrast to Peter and the disciples who "forsook all and followed him" and who will be rewarded accordingly in the coming kingdom, many like this rich man who are FIRST will be LAST to enter in and will do so with difficulty. In this man's case, he will have to change his priorities regarding material wealth, and it will be like a camel going through the eye of the needle. **But with God's help and the master plan he devised, the rich man will eventually get there; he will just be one of the last to enter in.**

What makes him one of the "first"? Let's look at the interaction between him and Jesus for our answer:

> *And, behold, one came and said unto him, Good Master, what good thing shall I do, that I may have eternal life? And he said unto him, Why callest thou me good? there is none good but one, that is, God: but if thou wilt enter into life, keep the commandments. He saith unto him, Which? Jesus said, Thou shalt do no murder, Thou shalt not commit adultery, Thou shalt not steal, Thou shalt not bear false witness, Honour thy father and thy mother: and, Thou shalt love thy neighbour as thyself. The young man saith unto him, All these*

Many Are Called but Few Chosen

things have I kept from my youth up: what lack I yet? (Matthew 19:16-20)

Did you ever wonder why Jesus was so straight in his response of verse 17? I know I did. He knew right from the start that this man's heart was not fully engaged in his commitment to the kingdom. Even though he had done all the works of righteous living, he had his deepest priorities elsewhere. He had been physically engaged in keeping the commandments from his **youth up**, indicating he had been serving God most of his life; therefore, he was one of the first to respond to the call *in terms of the point in his life when he did so*. But he had greater allegiance to other things, and the works alone were not going to be enough. The Lord wanted his entire heart, soul, mind, and strength.

The next verse in our study comes in Matthew 20:16:

So the last shall be first, and the first last: for many be called, but few chosen. (Matthew 20:16)

The word "so" could be stated any of the following ways: "in this manner," "on this wise," or "thus." The Passion Translation renders it this way:

Now you can understand what I meant when I said that the first will end up last and the last will end up being first. Everyone is invited, but few are the chosen. (Matthew 20:16)

It is interesting to note that all that comes between this verse and the other occurrence of the similar phrase in Matthew 19:30 is one parable. Does this parable communicate that all enter in and that it is just a matter of order only?

Jesus starts off by telling us that this parable is an example of the kingdom of heaven:

For the kingdom of heaven is like unto a man that is an householder, which went out early in the morning to hire labourers into his vineyard. (Matthew 20:1)

In this story, the owner of the vineyard hires laborers first thing in the morning and then in the third, sixth, ninth, and eleventh hours. The workers in the *first* group are promised a specific amount for their labor, while the rest are simply told that their remuneration would be "whatsoever is right."

Let's pick it up in verse 8:

So when even was come, the lord of the vineyard saith unto his steward, Call the labourers, and give them their hire, beginning from the last unto

> *the first. And when they came that were hired about the eleventh hour, they received every man a penny. (Matthew 20:8–9)*

Note that the rewards were given starting with the "last" and ending with the "first," and that they all received the same amount of pay. The "last" therefore are "first" to receive the reward for their labor, and the "first" are the "last" to be rewarded.

> *But when the first came, they supposed that they should have received more; and they likewise received every man a penny. And when they had received it, they murmured against the goodman of the house, Saying, These last have wrought but one hour, and thou hast made them equal unto us, which have borne the burden and heat of the day. (Matthew 20:10–12)*

It seems pretty clear: All the workers eventually receive the same reward for their labor; it is a matter of order only.

One of the main points in this story is the attitude of the first who end up being last. They felt that they should receive more because they labored longer than the rest—their whole lifetimes—as opposed to later in life after living contrary for most of it. Jesus confronted their attitude:

> But he answered one of them, and said, **Friend,** I do thee no wrong: didst not thou agree with me for a penny? Take that thine is, and go thy way: I will give unto this last, even as unto thee. Is it not lawful for me to do what I will with mine own? Is thine eye evil, because I am good? So the last shall be first, and the first last: for many be called, but few chosen. (Matthew 20:13–16)

Those who were first to enter into the labor in the vineyard focused more on their efforts than on the goodness of the master. That is the lesson Jesus was teaching in this record. Notice the term he used in verse 13 when addressing one of the individuals in the group: ***friend.***

This is the same term Jesus used in the upcoming usage of weeping and gnashing of teeth in Matthew 22, so it ties directly into that record. Jesus did not use words haphazardly or randomly; therefore, the two individuals in these records share a similar lesson to be learned.

> And when the king came in to see the guests, he saw there a man which had not on a wedding garment: And he saith unto him, **Friend,** how camest thou in hither not having a wedding garment? And he

was speechless. Then said the king to the servants, Bind him hand and foot, and take him away, and cast him into outer darkness, there shall be weeping and gnashing of teeth. For many are called, but few are chosen. (Matthew 22:11–14)

The gentleman in this record was called but not chosen because he was not dressed properly. If we add the teaching from the parable in Matthew 20, this gentleman was also more focused on his efforts and his time spent than he was on the goodness of the master. Therefore, he had some work to do to get his heart in the right place before he would be able to enter the wedding and to gain access to eternal salvation in the kingdom of the Messiah.

The problem with these two subjects from the different parables is that the individuals endeavored to enter into the kingdom based on their own works. Could it be that the missing clothing of Matthew 22 was the righteousness that the master provided, which can be acquired only by believing? This would fit with both records as well as the rich man in chapter 19. It would also indicate why many of the called were not chosen and why many of the first would be last. The "friends" in these two parables might have been halfheartedly involved most of their lives. However, they would need to ferret through their works-oriented approach to the kingdom before they will be willing to simply accept the gift the master desires for them. There will be some weeping and gnashing of teeth involved. Allow me to continue to make my case.

Between our last record in Matthew 20:16 and the parable in Matthew 22, a number of events are listed that do not contribute to our study. They include the trip to Jerusalem that Jesus took with his disciples, his foretelling of his death and resurrection, his teaching on servant leadership, his healing of the two blind men, his preparation for the Passover, and his first and second entrances into Jerusalem and the events therein.

We will pick up with the record in Matthew 21 that took place during Jesus' second visit into Jerusalem. There, he challenged and then confronted the logic of the chief priests and elders of the people:

> *But what think ye? A certain man had two sons; and he came to the first, and said, Son, go work to day in my vineyard. He answered and said, I will not: but afterward he repented, and went. And he came to the second, and said likewise. And he answered and said, I go, sir: and went not. (Matthew 21:28–30)*

The two sons were called to enter into **the labor in the vineyard**. The first son the father called to the work initially refused, but *afterward* he changed his mind and went. He would represent one of the "last" to enter into the labor in the vineyard, but because he had a change of heart, he would be one of the first to enter into the rewards of the kingdom.

The second son gave lip service to the father, indicating that he would enter *immediately* into the vineyard. There is no indication that this son ever actually commenced the true labor of the father, nor is there any mention of him later having a change of heart. He is an example of one who "enters into the labor" from the first, although it is not from the heart, and therefore he would not enter into the eternal salvation in the Messiah's kingdom until later as he has some repentance yet ahead of him.

Jesus then asked the disciples a question to see if they followed the logic:

Whether of them twain did the will of his father? They say unto him, The first. (Matthew 21:31)

They got it! They saw the truth behind the parable; however, they did not recognize its application to their lives. Jesus responded by spelling it out for them, and it couldn't have been any clearer:

*Jesus saith unto them, Verily I say unto you, That the publicans and the harlots go into the kingdom of God **before** you. (Matthew 21:31)*

There you have it! The publicans and harlots who lived a good part of their lives before repenting and entering into the labor will enter into the kingdom of God BEFORE the religious leaders who spent their lives in an outward appearance of the work. So many records come to mind when the truth comes to light. Many were called during Jesus' lifetime, but only a few were chosen because not everyone was willing to make the changes necessary to wholeheartedly enter into the labor.

This was similar to the rich man from the beginning of this study, who had kept all the commandments from his youth, but he still had some heart issues that he was not willing to deal with. His affections were set more on physical acquisitions than the kingdom of God, and he was unwilling to change when Jesus confronted him. He would eventually make it into the kingdom because God made a way, but it would be with hardship and weeping and gnashing of teeth.

Many of "the first" like this man, as well as the religious leaders Jesus confronted in the temple, had an outward appearance of service most of their lives, but they would be the last to be rewarded with entrance into the kingdom because their hearts were never fully involved. And many of the last to enter into the work, who were involved in other things at first (harlots and publicans, fishermen and doctors), would be the first to enter into the kingdom because they changed their minds and then truly labored with their whole hearts.

Now tying this all together, we have the following progression of truth:

- Many who are first shall be last, and the last shall be first (or the last shall be first and the first last) is another way of saying:
- Many are called but few are chosen, **which is another way of communicating the truth from the parable of Matthew 22.**
- Then said the king to the servants, Bind him hand and foot, and take him away, and cast him into outer darkness, there shall be weeping and gnashing of teeth.

In the context of the fourth occurrence of weeping and gnashing of teeth in Matthew 22, Jesus taught the same truth three different ways to make sure we would get the message. Those who had been raised in an outward form of service to God most of their lives he referred to as **"the called but not chosen."** They are the ones who think they should have an immediate entrée into his kingdom in the future because they were *first* to "enter into the labor," but they will need to do some inner heart changing; therefore, they will actually be the *last* to enter in. These individuals will need to recognize that their entrance into the eternal salvation in the kingdom of the Messiah will not be by their own efforts, but by the goodness of the master who made a way when there was none.

All of these truths are pieces of a puzzle that, when properly fit together, bring into focus the overall picture Jesus was communicating, that the state of "weeping and gnashing of teeth in outer darkness" is only temporary.

Who then are "the called" who are the "few who *are* chosen"? They would be the ones such as Peter and the disciples, the publicans and the harlots, who entered into the labor. They made the necessary changes in their hearts in this life. They chose to live in the context of the future and truly set their affections on the things of God by repenting and seeking forgiveness, even if not right from the start. They may have been the last to "enter into the work," but because their hearts were affected and they recognized it was all the master's doing and not their own, they are clothed in the righteousness that he provided. They will also be the first to enter into the kingdom coming for them in the future.

---

*A Critical Lexicon and Concordance to the English and Greek New Testament, page 296.

14

The Day of Christ and the Day of the Lord

I WILL NOW set before you a timeline that puts all the relevant events into perspective. Once again, I present this for your consideration, believing that it is necessary to fully communicate the subject matter of this book.

To start, I suggest that the reign of the king from heaven or the kingdom of heaven should be divided into two parts. The first part is recorded in the Gospels of the life and teachings of Jesus Christ, which took place about 2,000 years ago. He made this distinction in his opening remarks at the synagogue in Nazareth as we studied earlier:

> *And he came to Nazareth, where he had been brought up: and, as his custom was, he went into the synagogue on the sabbath day, and stood up for to read. And there was delivered unto him the book of the prophet Esaias. And when he had opened the book, he found the place where it was written, The Spirit of the Lord is upon me, because he hath anointed me to preach the gospel to the*

poor; he hath sent me to heal the brokenhearted, to preach deliverance to the captives, and recovering of sight to the blind, to set at liberty them that are bruised, **To preach the acceptable year of the Lord.** *And he closed the book, and he gave it again to the minister, and sat down. And the eyes of all them that were in the synagogue were fastened on him. (Luke 4:16–20)*

Jesus intentionally read only the first phrase of Isaiah 61:2. He then stopped, rolled up the scroll, gave it back to the minister, and sat down. Why? And why was everyone watching with rapt attention?

And then he made the following decree:

And he began to say unto them, **This day is this scripture fulfilled** *in your ears. (Luke 4:21)*

Surely those who awaited the Messiah and who knew the Old Testament scriptures concerning him were hanging on each word as he quoted this familiar text from Isaiah 61. When he stopped in the middle of verse 2, they had had their eyes fastened on him, waiting for him to finish. But he didn't. Why?

The Spirit of the Lord G<small>OD</small> *is upon me; because the* L<small>ORD</small> *hath anointed me to preach good tidings*

The Day of Christ and the Day of the Lord

> *unto the meek; he hath sent me to bind up the brokenhearted, to proclaim liberty to the captives, and the opening of the prison to them that are bound; To proclaim the acceptable year of the* Lord, **and the day of vengeance of our God;** *to comfort all that mourn. (Isaiah 61:1-2)*

Why did he stop right in the **middle** of verse 2 and communicate that this prophecy was being fulfilled that very day? He did so to make the distinction that the second part of his "mission," "the day of vengeance of our God," **the day when God would make things right,** by contrast would not be unfolding at that time.

In so doing, our Lord divided his ministry on earth into two phases: the acceptable year of the Lord, which he was proclaiming had come; and the day of vengeance of our God, which would happen at some point in the future. Not understanding this distinction has caused much confusion regarding future events.

This subject was still on the minds of the disciples and came up again on the day of the Ascension, right before he departed into heaven:

> *When they therefore were come together, they asked of him, saying, Lord, wilt thou at this time* **restore again the kingdom to Israel?** *And he said unto them, It is not for you to know* **the times or**

> ***the seasons**, which the Father hath put in his own power. (Acts 1:6-7)*

This is the very last question recorded of the disciples to Jesus before he ascended. They were still looking for the fulfillment of Old Testament prophecies on how he would make things right and restore the kingdom to Israel. In a sense, they were saying to him: "Ahem, uh Jesus, aren't you forgetting something?" He told them that it was not for them to know, and he referred to it as **"the times or the seasons."** He then redirected them to the commissioning they would need to attend to at that particular time:

> ***But** ye shall receive power, after that the Holy Ghost is come upon you: and ye shall be witnesses unto me both in Jerusalem, and in all Judaea, and in Samaria, and unto the uttermost part of the earth. (Acts 1:8)*

The disciples were still expecting Jesus to fulfill all the Old Testament prophecies and restore the kingdom to Israel the first time around, but he had already made it clear from his proclamation back in Nazareth that this was not going to be the case. That future period, which Isaiah referred to as "the day of vengeance of our God," Jesus referred to as "the times or the seasons."

The Day of Christ and the Day of the Lord

Paul used a similar phrase in his first epistle to the Thessalonians:

*But of the **times and the seasons**, brethren, ye have no need that I write unto you. (1 Thessalonians 5:1)*

Paul described a time that they did not need him to write about. This is basically the same thing Jesus told his disciples on the day of the Ascension. Could it be they were referring to the same time period?

*For yourselves know perfectly that **the day of the Lord** so cometh as a thief in the night. (1 Thessalonians 5:2)*

In the next verse, Paul introduced the "day of the Lord" in this context. The grammatical construction of these two verses equates the "times and the seasons" with the "day of the Lord." If this "day" WAS something the Thessalonian church would be going through, and it would come as a thief in the night, then why would there be *no need* to have anything written about it? You would think the opposite would be true.

Putting all this together, the conclusion is simple: the period that Jesus referred to as the "times **or** the seasons" and Paul called the "times **and** the seasons," also referred to as the day of the Lord when "vengeance" will be administered by Jesus and the kingdom restored to Israel, *is a time that the church would not need instruction about in his absence.*

> *For when **they** shall say, Peace and safety; then sudden destruction cometh upon **them**, as travail upon a woman with child; and **they** shall not escape. (1 Thessalonians 5:3)*

It is interesting to note how verse 3, which describes the time just prior to the "day of the Lord," speaks in the third person with the pronouns "they" and "them." This event will take place when the individuals think everything is OK, when in reality it will be just the opposite. No wonder it was a concern that Paul had to address. This would not be a good time to be around, and the idea that the Thessalonian church would have to go through it was spreading among the believers, causing great fear. But these events will occur at the end of the tribulation when darkness will rule with the antichrist at the helm and the "seed of the serpent" in positions of authority across the globe. Praise God that the church we belong to does not need anything written about it, because thanks to the Lord Jesus Christ, *we will not be included among those subject to that reign of the enemy*!

The Day of Christ and the Day of the Lord

> ***But** ye, brethren, are not in darkness, that that day should overtake you as a thief. Ye are all the **children** of light, and the children of the day: we are not of the night, nor of darkness. (1 Thessalonians 5:4–5)*

There is another big "but" at the beginning of verse 4. We the church, during the age of Grace who are born again, are not in darkness, **nor will we be in the future during what will be the darkest hour of history**, but indeed we are **children** of light and of the day.

> *Therefore let us not sleep, as do others; but let us watch and be sober. For they that sleep sleep in the night; and they that be drunken are drunken in the night. But let us, who are of the day, be sober, putting on the breastplate of faith and love; and for an helmet, the hope of salvation. (1 Thessalonians 5:6–8)*

Then comes this exhortation: Since we are children of the day and light, let's live like it! We should walk in faith and love. Knowing now that we will not go through the dark times to come, we all have a helmet to protect our heads and indeed our very thought lives, knowing the **hope of our salvation**! What an amazing God! What an awesome Savior!

*For God hath not appointed us to **wrath**, but to obtain salvation by our Lord Jesus Christ. (1 Thessalonians 5:9)*

How interesting that in this context, the concept of wrath comes up and the Thessalonians are told they were not appointed or going to be brought into it. Furthermore, the verse does not say whose wrath it is speaking of, and yet many of the translators attribute it to God, and in so doing bring their theology into the interpretation. Could this be the "wrath" or intense passion of another source? The whole context of this section of scripture is darkness: that which we are to avoid as "children of light and the day," and that which will obscure "the day of the Lord" for those upon whom it will come as a "thief in the night." Does this sound like something that would be associated with a loving, kind, and forgiving Father? Or is there another source?

The other two occurrences of this truth that we are not going to experience the darkest time of all history, do not list a source for the wrath either:

*Much more then, being now justified by his blood, we shall be saved from **wrath** through him. (Romans 5:9)*

The Day of Christ and the Day of the Lord

*And to wait for his Son from heaven, whom he raised from the dead, even Jesus, which delivered us from the **wrath** to come. (1 Thessalonians 1:10)*

This is not the wrath of the Lord Jesus Christ either, or the wording would be different. In both verses, Jesus is the subject. Romans 5:9 would say something more along the lines of "We shall be saved from HIS wrath through him." In the same manner, 1 Thessalonians 1:10 would more accurately read, "Delivered us from HIS wrath to come."

No, this time that is yet to come about which the church needs nothing to be written about is NOT the manifestation of the anger of God, but it is the unrestrained evil and lust of the dark one unleashing his intense passion across the earth. The Lord Jesus Christ will save us from this "wrath" of the devil to come, which we will develop further in this chapter.

Now that we have presented the case that "the day of the Lord" is a future event and indeed the second part of Jesus' mission on earth, we are going to be looking at the distinctions between it and what is known as the "day of Christ." Although on the surface these two days may seem similar, as we dig into the details, you will see that they are two separate events that have been mistakenly viewed as one, resulting in much confusion throughout history. Once again they are:

- The return of the Lord Jesus FOR his church, known as **gathering together** or **the rapture**, which occurs at the end of the grace administration and is referred to as **the day of Christ**;

AND

- The return of the Lord Jesus Christ WITH his church, known as the **day of vengeance of our God**, which occurs at the end of the tribulation and is referred to as **the day of the Lord**.

"The day of" can be understood in a broader sense to mean the "return of" or "visitation from." In the next chapter, we will also look at a third "day" that has been overlooked by most, but is an event that has the greatest impact on our understanding of how the future unfolds and specifically the events recorded beginning in Revelation 20.

For now, consider the following verses addressed to the church from the epistle to the Philippians:

*Being confident of this very thing, that he which hath begun a good work in you will perform it until the **day of Jesus Christ**. (Philippians 1:6)*

The Day of Christ and the Day of the Lord

*That ye may approve things that are excellent; that ye may be sincere and without offence till the **day of Christ**. (Philippians 1:10)*

*Holding forth the word of life; that I may rejoice in the **day of Christ**, that I have not run in vain, neither laboured in vain. (Philippians 2:16)*

The preceding verses use the phrase "day of Christ" as an ending point, either clearly or inferred. This "day" will mark the end of the "grace administration." This event is most clearly laid out in 1 Thessalonians chapter 4:

For if we believe that Jesus died and rose again, even so them also which sleep in Jesus will God bring with him. For this we say unto you by the word of the Lord, that we which are alive and remain unto the coming of the Lord shall not prevent them which are asleep. For the Lord himself shall descend from heaven with a shout, with the voice of the archangel, and with the trump of God: and the dead in Christ shall rise first: Then we which are alive and remain shall be caught up together with them in the clouds, to meet the Lord in the air: and so shall we ever be with the Lord. Wherefore comfort one another with these words. (1 Thessalonians 4:14–18)

It is interesting to note that the "day of the Lord" as described in chapter 5 immediately follows and is **contrasted** with this event:

> **But** *of the times and the seasons, brethren, ye have no need that I write unto you. For yourselves know perfectly that the day of the Lord so cometh as a thief in the night. (1 Thessalonians 5:1-2)*

The "times and seasons," which is the "day of the Lord" described in the rest of the chapter, is not the same as the gathering together, the rapture, or the "day of Christ."

The second book of Thessalonians draws distinctions and contrasts between these two events as well:

> *Now we beseech you, brethren, by the coming of our Lord Jesus Christ, and by our gathering together unto him. (2 Thessalonians 2:1)*

This verse sets the context for what is to follow. Here are some other translations in which it is much clearer:

> *Now **in regard to** the coming of our Lord Jesus Christ and our gathering together to meet Him, we ask you, brothers and sisters. (Amplified)*

The Day of Christ and the Day of the Lord

> *Now **concerning** the coming of our Lord Jesus Christ and our being gathered to him: We ask you, brothers and sisters. (Christian Standard Bible)*

> *Brothers and sisters, we have **something to say about** the coming of our Lord Jesus Christ. We want to talk to you **about that time when** we will meet together with him. (Easy-to-Read Version)*

You get the idea. What will follow are truths regarding the gathering together of the church, which is the day of Christ. The next two verses have introduced much confusion into the distinction between this day and the day of the Lord.

> *That ye be not soon shaken in mind, or be troubled, neither by spirit, nor by word, nor by letter as from us, as that the **day of Christ** is at hand. Let no man deceive you by any means: for that day shall not come, except there come **a falling away** first, and that man of sin be revealed, the son of perdition. (2 Thessalonians 2:2–3)*

I would first like to address the usage of "the day of Christ" in verse 2. The word "Christ" is actually "Lord" in six out of the seven critical Greek texts. Now this section makes a little more sense. Paul is telling them by revelation not to freak out by any message coming from any source that the day of vengeance of the Lord has come. This is the same message he set forth in 1 Thessalonians 5.

He then goes on to say that that day will not come until there is a certain event first, which is listed in verse 3. The King James Version translates it as "a falling away," and it has been rendered in other translations as "rebellion, turning away, revolt, rejection, and apostasy." I have always had a problem with those interpretations. The wording in verses 2 and 3 is very clear, adamant, and unequivocal: No matter where the message comes from, we are not to be deceived by any means, for that day absolutely shall not come until **this event**, which will have to be something undeniable and indisputable to fit in the context.

It could have been said many times in history that there was "a great apostasy." How about the Dark Ages, for instance? Some may even think this is happening today. But there is a completely different line of thought that the church is actually rallying and uniting with an understanding of the power we wield, more than ever before. No, the event referred to in this passage is completely outside the realm of man's doing—it is actually referring to the gathering together as set forth in verse 1.

The Day of Christ and the Day of the Lord

The Greek word used in the original text for "falling away" is *apostasia*. The term "apostasy" is derived from it, and it is rendered as such in many translations. Please consider the possibility that this word has been changed semantically over the years. It is used in only one other place in the New Testament, in Acts 21:21. Look at these translations:

> *Now they have heard of thee that thou teachest those Jews, who are among the Gentiles, to **depart** from Moses. (Douay-Rheims 1899 American Edition)*

> *They have ·heard [been informed] about your teaching, that you tell ·our people [the Jews] who live among the ·nations [Gentiles] to **leave** the law of Moses [forsake/abandon Moses]. (Expanded Bible)*

> *These Jews have heard about your teaching. They heard that you tell the Jews who live among non-Jews to **leave** the law of Moses. (International Children's Bible)*

> *They have heard about your teaching, that you tell our people who live among the nations to **leave** the law of Moses. (New Century Version)*

*They have heard about you. They have heard you teach the Jews who live among people who are not Jews. They have heard you teach them to **break away** from the Law of Moses. (New Life Version)*

*And they heard of thee, that thou teachest **departing** from Moses of those Jews that be by heathen men. (Wycliffe Bible)*

What if the correct translation of 2 Thessalonians 2:3 should be "departing," "breaking away," or "leaving"? That translation is well within the bounds of the word as illustrated. Consider the following three translations that preceded the King James version:

*Let no man deceiue you by any meanes: for that day shall not come, except there come a **departing** first, and that that man of sinne be disclosed, euen the sonne of perdition, (Geneva Bible of 1587)*

*Let noman disceaue you by eny meanes. For the LORDE commeth not, excepte **the departynge** come first, and that that Man of synne be opened, euen the sonne of perdicion, (Coverdale Bible of 1535).*

The Day of Christ and the Day of the Lord

*Let no ma deceave you by eny meanes for the lorde commeth not excepte ther come **a departynge** fyrst and that that synfnll man be opened ye sonne of perdicion (Tyndale Bible of 1526)*

And the following recent version as well:

*Let no one deceive you in any way. For it will not be, unless **the departure** comes first, and the man of sin is revealed, the son of destruction, (World English Bible)*

Now let's look at the rest of the context to see how it would flow with that rendering.

*Let no man deceive you by any means: for that day shall not come, except there come a falling away **[the departing or the departure]** first, and that man of sin be revealed, the son of perdition; Who opposeth and exalteth himself above all that is called God, or that is worshipped; so that he as God sitteth in the temple of God, shewing himself that he is God. Remember ye not, that, when I was yet with you, I told you these things? And now ye know what **withholdeth** that he might be revealed in his time. For the mystery of iniquity doth already* *work: only he who now **letteth** will **let**, until he be taken out of the way. (2 Thessalonians 2:3-7)*

The words translated ***"withholdeth," "letteth,"*** and ***"let"*** are all derivatives of the same word in the Greek text. In his *Lexicon of Greek Words*, E.W. Bullinger defines the word as "to have and hold down, hold fast, restrain."* This does indeed fit, telling us that the son of perdition or the antichrist will not rise to power until the church—which holds him down, holds him fast, and restrains him—is "taken out of the way," the third reference to the gathering together.

Now that we have a potential rendering of the first seven verses in 2 Thessalonians, we not only have a clear distinction between the day of Christ and the day of the Lord, but we also have an order of future events. The next event to take place will be the gathering together of the church of the body, the day of Christ, which will mark the end of the grace administration. After that point, the antichrist will no longer be restrained and will rise to power, indicating that the tribulation will begin.

The greater context of this chapter was addressing the concern that was spreading through the Thessalonian church that the day of the Lord was upon them. Paul taught them not to believe that, no matter who tried to tell them. He explained that it would absolutely not happen until they would depart first, which would trigger

The Day of Christ and the Day of the Lord

the time of the tribulation, and that these events would take place before the day of the Lord. Therefore, it can be concluded that the day of the Lord will take place after the tribulation.

> *Then the lawless one [the Antichrist] will be revealed and the Lord Jesus will slay him with the breath of His mouth and bring him to an end by the appearance of His coming.* (2 Thessalonians 2:8 Amplified Bible)

This glorious event, "the day of the Lord," will mark the beginning of the millennial kingdom when Jesus will make everything right and restore the kingdom to Israel, among many other events yet unfulfilled.

---

*A Critical Lexicon and Concordance to the English and Greek New Testament, page 891.

15

The Day of God

SO FAR, WE have looked at the day of Christ and the day of the Lord, with the intent to show the distinctions between the two. The understanding set forth was that these days are the coming or visitation of the entity they are associated with. The day of Christ will be when Jesus Christ comes back to gather his church. The day of the Lord will be when the Lord Jesus Christ comes back **with** the church to establish the millennial kingdom and to set everything straight.

There is another day in the Word of God that has not received the same attention as the first two. It is my belief that the understanding of this day is critical to building and supporting the subject of this book. It will address what happens at the end of time, including the lake of fire in Revelation, which is the furnace of fire Jesus taught about in the Gospels. It will put everything into proper perspective, showing that God does not change his nature of love at that point in history:

> But the **day of the Lord** will come as a thief in the night; in the which the heavens shall pass away

> *with a great noise, and the elements shall melt with fervent heat, the earth also and the works that are therein shall be burned up. (2 Peter 3:10)*

This event is referred to as "the day of the Lord." Is this referring to the **Lord Jesus Christ**, and if so, is it just another record about the events unfolding at the end of the tribulation? If that is our understanding, we will have multiple problems reconciling the activity recorded here with the other events of that day.

On this particular day, the heavens will pass with a great noise, the elements will melt with fervent heat, and the earth and the works therein will be burned up. How will the Lord Jesus set up his millennial kingdom on earth if it is burned up? Now I have lots of confusion and multiple questions, and we are off into many different tangents and theologies.

What if this is indeed a separate event altogether and not referring to the Lord Jesus Christ specifically? Could this event actually be referring to the end of time and the lake and furnace of fire? Let's read on:

> *Seeing then that all these things shall be dissolved, what manner of persons ought ye to be in all holy conversation and godliness. (2 Peter 3:11)*

The Day of God

Since everything we see around us in the physical realm will be gone at this point, how much sense does it make to live our lives for it alone in the context of eternity?

*Looking for and hasting unto the coming of the day of **God**, wherein the heavens being on fire shall be dissolved, and the elements shall melt with fervent heat? (2 Peter 3:12)*

The subject of this day is the Lord **God**, and the word for God, *theos*, is used in every critical Greek text. This is indeed a different day altogether. This is a day when God himself in all his glory comes back to be with mankind, which was his passion all along. He knew the impact that his presence would have on the creation, when perfect light would enter a creation that had been infiltrated by darkness.

This then is the message which we have heard of him, and declare unto you, that God is light, and in him is no darkness at all. (1 John 1:5)

It can be seen in the physical realm that light and darkness cannot occupy the same space at the same time. In the darkest cave, a single match will prevail. When the sun rises in the morning, the darkness of night is overcome. Yet we cannot stare at that source of light without significant physical harm. That light is not perfect, and shadows remain in its presence.

Look at the effects of the light or glory of the Lord Jesus Christ:

And as he journeyed, he came near Damascus: and suddenly there shined round about him a light from heaven: And Saul arose from the earth; and when his eyes were opened, he saw no man: but they led him by the hand, and brought him into Damascus. And he was three days without sight, and neither did eat nor drink. (Acts 9:3, 8–9)

Later, when he recounted this story to King Agrippa, he added the following detail:

At midday, O king, I saw in the way a light from heaven, **above the brightness of the sun***, shining round about me and them which journeyed with me. (Acts 26:13)*

The light from heaven that accompanied this visitation of the Lord Jesus Christ was enough to blind Paul for three days. The glory of the Lord Jesus Christ at his return will have a significant impact on the kingdom of

The Day of God

darkness, and it will be the source of the first lake of fire recorded in the book of Revelation.

> *And then shall that Wicked be revealed, whom the Lord shall consume with the spirit of his mouth, and shall destroy with **the brightness of his coming**. (2 Thessalonians 2:8)*

> *And I saw the beast, and the kings of the earth, and their armies, gathered together to make war against him that sat on the horse, and against his army. And the beast was taken, and with him the false prophet that wrought miracles before him, with which he deceived them that had received the mark of the beast, and them that worshipped his image. These both were cast alive into a **lake of fire burning with brimstone**. (Revelation 19:19–20)*

These two records describe the same event in different terms. It is the day of the Lord where Jesus comes to set up his millennial kingdom. He will set everything right and fulfill all the prophecies of the Old Testament that he didn't during his first earthly ministry. It is the day of vengeance of our God that he did not mention when reading from Isaiah chapter 61 in his address to the synagogue in Nazareth.

The day of God, on the other hand, will bring about glory that will completely set darkness ablaze throughout all creation. It will be the perfection of light where absolutely no darkness can exist.

Moses in the Old Testament had a relationship with God that was singularly significant. He asked if he could see God's glory during one of his intimate encounters with the Lord:

> *And he said, I beseech thee, shew me thy glory. And he said, I will make all my goodness pass before thee, and I will proclaim the name of the* Lord *before thee; and will be gracious to whom I will be gracious, and will shew mercy on whom I will shew mercy. And he said, Thou canst not see my face: for* **there shall no man see me, and live.** *(Exodus 33:18–20)*

Moses asked to see the glory of God, and he in response said no man could see his face. Why is it that no man can see God's face and live? Is it because our sin seperates us from him as some believe? This was a statement from God to Moses just nine verses earlier:

> *And the* Lord *spake unto Moses face to face, as a man speaketh unto his friend. (Exodus 33:11)*

The Day of God

Moses had a unique and intimate relationship with God already, as the scriptures bear out and as this verse figuratively communicates. If he was unable to see God's face and live, there must be more to it. Could the reason be the darkness that has entered into the world and into the very nature of man as a result of Adam's fall? God is perfect light, and darkness to any degree cannot exist in his presence.

> *That thou keep this commandment without spot, unrebukable, until the appearing of our Lord Jesus Christ: Which in his times he shall shew, who is the blessed and only Potentate, the King of kings, and Lord of lords; Who only hath immortality,* ***dwelling in the light which no man can approach unto***; *whom no man hath seen,* **nor can see**: *to whom be honour and power everlasting. Amen. (1 Timothy 6:14–16)*

Jesus Christ, God's only begotten Son who lived perfectly and always did his will, is the only one to ever dwell in the very presence of God's perfect light and glory. He has made a way for mankind to have access as well.

> *For I know nothing by myself; yet am I not hereby justified: but he that judgeth me is the Lord.*

> *Therefore judge nothing before the time, until the Lord come, who both will **bring to light the hidden things of darkness**, and will make manifest the counsels of the hearts: and then shall every man have praise of God. (1 Corinthians 4:4-5)*

This was the purpose of Jesus Christ's ministry, to separate light from darkness so that when God did come in his dazzling glory, those who chose light would be able to exist in his very presence. For those who do not choose to respond to the calling the first time, they will have a **second chance** in the future, so they will be equipped for this event at the end of time. For those of us who have already chosen, we are already prepared:

> *To whom God would make known what is the riches of the glory of this mystery among the Gentiles; which is Christ in you, **the hope of glory**. (Colossians 1:27)*

In this context, let's look at a few of the scripture pieces that have already come up in our study and see if they make even more sense now that the puzzle is coming together.

> *What if God, willing to shew his wrath, and to make his power known, endured with much*

The Day of God

*longsuffering the **vessels of wrath fitted to destruction**: And that he might make known the riches of his glory on the **vessels of mercy, which he had afore prepared unto glory**. (Romans 9:22–23)*

This one event, at the end of time, the return of the Almighty God in all his glory will have two outcomes. Those who have already chosen God's archenemy as the true lord have eternally aligned themselves with darkness and therefore will burst into flames and be destroyed. God will take no pleasure in this whatsoever. However, everyone else who has chosen the Lord Jesus Christ, through the mercy of God, is prepared for this event.

Jesus taught it this way as we saw while working through the weeping and gnashing series:

*As therefore the tares are gathered and burned in the fire; so shall it be in the end of this world. The Son of man shall send forth his angels, and they shall gather out of his kingdom all things that offend, and them which do iniquity; And shall cast them into **a furnace of fire**: there shall be wailing and gnashing of teeth. **Then shall the righteous shine forth as the sun** in the kingdom of their Father. Who hath ears to hear, let him hear. (Matthew 13:40–43)*

Are you beginning to see the pattern? The one event at the end of time is just a loving heavenly Father whose passion to be with mankind has been overflowing inside him ever since the Fall. He chose to wait until all of humanity would have a chance, and for many a second chance to choose what side of this event they would land on. For all those who made the right choice, the outcome is called glorification, with the result being our "shining as the sun."

> *For whom he did foreknow, he also did predestinate to be conformed to the image of his Son, that he might be the firstborn among many brethren. Moreover whom he did predestinate, them he also called: and whom he called, them he also justified: and whom he justified, them he also* **glorified**. *(Romans 8:29–30)*

Oh, what a glorious day that will be!

16

Conclusion

AS I CONCLUDE the message I have attempted to communicate, allow me to remind you that my goal was not to cover every single verse on each of the topics presented. This was never intended to be an exhaustive work on the subject because I did not want it to be a 400-page treatise. What I tried to do was to lay out a framework with enough scripture to support it that would provide a system of truths spanning the Bible that would lead to a clearer picture of the events yet to come.

It is my hope that you will take the time to search these things out for yourself to see if the overall picture might be accurate. I always think of the Bereans in this context:

> *These were more noble than those in Thessalonica, in that they received the word with all readiness of mind, and searched the scriptures daily, whether those things were so. Therefore many of them believed; also of honourable women which were Greeks, and of men, not a few. (Acts 17:11–12)*

Notice that it says that they received the word with all *readiness of mind*, and then they searched the scriptures daily to see if those things were so. If you start from the place of opposition, without even considering what is presented, your search of the scriptures will be colored by your established viewpoint.

I have put off finalizing this work for many years, because I would never want to teach something that was not accurate. However, every time I have come across a section from scripture regarding the end times, it has always fit within the boundaries of the "puzzle box" I have set before you.

In the fifteen prior chapters, my primary goal was to set before you two overall perspectives. First, God is love; therefore, his nature does not allow the anger and wrath that have been attributed to him in the context of the days to come. Second, only two categories of people will be at the very end of time. There has always been so much confusion as to what happens to the unsaved. I believe the confusion exists because the Bible does not address a third group, simply because there won't be one. By the end of time, there will be only the children of the kingdom and the children of the wicked one.

Throughout this book, I continued to point out the dichotomy in the Word of God regarding those two classifications of people in the end, starting with the first prophecy in Genesis 3:15 and ending with the two

Conclusion

resurrections. We looked at those two classifications in the study of "weeping and gnashing of teeth." Regarding the first resurrection, we saw the connection between "the children of the kingdom" and the truth that "many of the first shall be last and the last shall be first," communicating that all will be saved in the end, but that it would take longer for some than others. The study in Romans 9–11 establishes this truth regarding Israel.

We also saw that a second category of humans will not participate in the first resurrection because God could do nothing for them. In this final chapter, having revealed a third and separate event known as the day of God, the intention will be to show that the furnace of fire they are destined for is not the outflow of an angry God, but it is merely the presence of him in all his glory and the impact it will have on darkness as a whole.

> *And I saw thrones, and they sat upon them, and judgment was given unto them: and I saw the souls of them that were beheaded for the witness of Jesus, and for the word of God, and **which** had not worshipped the beast, neither his image, neither had received his mark upon their foreheads, or in their hands; and they lived and reigned with Christ a thousand years. (Revelation 20:4)*

This verse describing the participants of the first resurrection is conclusive on its own, when we understand that the proper interpretation of the word "which" should be "whosoever." After additional supporting truths, the case was made that the participants in the first resurrection would range from the martyrs all the way to those who ***did not*** commit the unforgiveable sin, and everyone in between. In our modern vernacular, we would say this very inclusive group is presented in terms of "from A to Z" or "from soup to nuts."

> *But the rest of the dead lived not again until the thousand years were finished. This is the first resurrection. (Revelation 20:5)*

If our premise regarding verse 4 holds true, then the "rest of the dead" are those who ***did*** commit the blasphemy against the Holy Spirit, and they will remain in the grave for the duration of the millennial kingdom. This verse also infers very clearly that they will be raised after the thousand years are over: "The rest of the dead lived not again until the thousand years were finished." This is another way of saying that the rest of the dead WILL live again after the thousand years expire.

In the same manner, when verse 6 gives attributes regarding those who will participate in the first resurrection, it is also telling us about those who won't:

Conclusion

Blessed and holy is he that hath part in the first resurrection: on such the second death hath no power, but they shall be priests of God and of Christ, and shall reign with him a thousand years. (Revelation 20:6)

Instead of being "blessed and holy," they are "cursed and unholy." They are the "cursed children" we looked at before starting with Cain in Genesis 4. They are the "unholy" of 2 Timothy 3:

*This know also, that in the last days perilous times shall come. For men shall be lovers of their own selves, covetous, boasters, proud, **blasphemers**, disobedient to parents, unthankful, **unholy**, Without natural affection, trucebreakers, false accusers, incontinent, fierce, despisers of those that are good. (2 Timothy 3:1-3)*

This prophecy of the "last days" gives us another list of attributes of these individuals. Notice that they are also called "blasphemers." Their final destination after they are raised from the dead will be a second established death and separation from God's ultimate plan for humanity. In that context, consider the following section of scripture from the book of Jude:

> *Woe unto them! for **they have gone in the way of Cain**, and ran greedily after the error of Balaam for reward, and perished in the gainsaying of Core.*
>
> *These are spots in your feasts of charity, when they feast with you, feeding themselves without fear: clouds they are without water, carried about of winds; trees whose fruit withereth, without fruit, **twice dead**, plucked up by the roots (Jude 11 and 12).*

Continuing on in the twentieth chapter of Revelation:

> *And when the thousand years are expired, Satan shall be loosed out of his prison. (Revelation 20:7)*

While it does not come right out and say it in this verse, as we concluded from verse 5, the cursed and unholy will also be raised from the dead at this point. Prior to this, Jesus will have had a full 1,000 years to reach all the unsaved, and will have achieved complete success in the end. That having been accomplished, the human element of deception will be raised for the final battle that began back in Genesis 3:15. This will be the final confrontation between light and darkness, the kingdom of God and the kingdom of the devil.

Conclusion

And shall go out to deceive the nations which are in the four quarters of the earth, Gog, and Magog, to gather them together to battle: the number of whom is as the sand of the sea. (Revelation 20:8)

If all those who were part of the millennial kingdom have been saved by this point, then who is the devil going out to deceive and gather together to battle? The answer is simple: those who were still in the grave during the 1,000 years, and who were just raised when he was loosed out of his prison. He is now rallying his troops for the final battle. Note that the objects of his deception are gathered from the four quarters of the earth. They are referred to as Gog and Magog, and in that context, consider the following from *The Companion Bible*:

> (Referring to Gog, it's noted): *"It marks the climax of Satan's effort to destroy Israel from being a people and clearly belongs to the close of a yet future kingdom age."*

> (Later in defining Magog): *If "Gog" denotes and symbolizes all that is powerful, gigantic, and proud, then "Magog" is symbolical of the same lands and peoples.**

In Revelation 20:8, it says that the number of this group is as the "sand of the sea." Most of the studies that I have read suggest that around 108 billion people were ever born. As an example only, and by no means intended to be a statement of truth, I've always used the following hypothesis: If only one out of every 100,000 people committed the blasphemy against the Holy Ghost, there would be 1,080,000 people advancing on the camp of the saints. Not to mention all those who would be "compelled to blaspheme" during the reign of the antichrist, which could very possibly vastly exceed that number.

The term "sand of the sea" is figurative, of course, and is used in the Bible to describe the children of Abraham as well as the children of Israel. However, it is also used in the following record:

And the Midianites and the Amalekites and all the children of the east lay along in the valley like grasshoppers for multitude; and their camels were without number, as the **sand by the sea side** *for multitude. (Judges 7:12)*

The phrase is a figure of speech that was in common use at the time. It means an impressive and formidable number, but is not meant to be taken literally. In Revelation 20:8, this sizable opponent, moving in a

Conclusion

coordinated effort as never seen before, along with the entire kingdom of darkness surrounding them, would be an intimidating sight, no matter how outnumbered they might be.

Then comes the ninth verse, which may now be seen in a new light (pardon the pun):

*And they went up on the breadth of the earth, and compassed the camp of the saints about, and the beloved city: and **fire came down from God out of heaven**, and devoured them. (Revelation 20:9)*

Here we see everyone else (those from the first resurrection) being referred to as "saints" and all gathered in one place referred to as their "camp." If this is a gathering of all those from the first resurrection and the "rest of the dead" from the second, then this will truly be an event where everyone who ever lived will be present. That being the case, the following scripture fits in and describes this "final act" of time:

*And **all flesh** shall see the salvation of God. (Luke 3:6)*

The prophet Isaiah put it this way:

Sinners in the Hands of a Loving God

> *And the glory of the* Lord *shall be revealed, and* ***all flesh*** *shall see it together: for the mouth of the* Lord *hath spoken it. (Isaiah 40:5)*

Everyone who has ever lived will be at this final showdown and will witness the salvation of God, the revelation of all his glory. This is the day of God where he returns to be with mankind because the lines have been drawn. Those who have committed themselves to darkness, both from the human and spiritual realms, along with the heavens and earth that have been affected by its permeation, will all burst into flames in the presence of perfect light.

This final act of God, his "magnum opus," his grand masterpiece, will be viewed by everyone who has ever lived. This is the one event that will have two outcomes: The vessels of wrath will see destruction, and the vessels of mercy will see glory. The children of the wicked one will be consumed in a lake of fire along with everything else that has been permeated by darkness, and those who have been saved, the rest of mankind, will be glorified and will shine as the sun.

This tremendous event is described in several ways in the remaining verses in the chapter.

> *And the devil that deceived them was cast into the lake of fire and brimstone,* ***where the beast and***

Conclusion

the false prophet are, *and shall be tormented day and night for ever and ever. (Revelation 20:10)*

The beast and the false prophet were already consumed by the glory of the Lord Jesus Christ upon his return, the day of the Lord, as depicted in Revelation 19:

And I saw heaven opened, and behold a white horse; and he that sat upon him was called Faithful and True, and in righteousness he doth judge and make war. His eyes were as a flame of fire, and on his head were many crowns; and he had a name written, that no man knew, but he himself. And he was clothed with a vesture dipped in blood: and his name is called The Word of God. And the armies which were in heaven followed him upon white horses, clothed in fine linen, white and clean. And out of his mouth goeth a sharp sword, that with it he should smite the nations: and he shall rule them with a rod of iron: and he treadeth the winepress of the fierceness and wrath of Almighty God. And he hath on his vesture and on his thigh a name written, KING OF KINGS, AND LORD OF LORDS.

And I saw an angel standing in the sun; and he cried with a loud voice, saying to all the fowls that fly in the midst of heaven, Come and gather yourselves together unto the supper of the great God; That ye may eat the flesh of kings, and the flesh of captains, and the flesh of mighty men, and the flesh of horses, and of them that sit on them, and the flesh of all men, both free and bond, both small and great. And I saw the beast, and the kings of the earth, and their armies, gathered together to make war against him that sat on the horse, and against his army. **And the beast was taken, and with him the false prophet that wrought miracles before him, with which he deceived them that had received the mark of the beast, and them that worshipped his image. These both were cast alive into a lake of fire burning with brimstone.** *And the remnant were slain with the sword of him that sat upon the horse, which sword proceeded out of his mouth: and all the fowls were filled with their flesh. (Revelation 19:11–21)*

This event is referred to as the battle of Armageddon when Jesus Christ and the born-again believers of the church of grace return at the end of the tribulation. They will triumph decisively over everything the antichrist built during his reign of terror. This event, the day of the Lord, is not the same as the day of God. Conflating the two has caused much confusion.

Conclusion

This is the first showdown, where the Lord Jesus Christ throws down the kingdom of the antichrist and sets up his millennial kingdom in its place. This event was described in 2 Thessalonians chapter 2:

*And then shall that Wicked be revealed, whom the Lord shall consume with the spirit of his mouth, and shall **destroy with the brightness of his coming**. (2 Thessalonians 2:8)*

What an amazing day that will be, when the truth will be made manifestly clear that the kingdom of the antichrist throughout history was never a match for the kingdom of the Lord Jesus Christ. In similar fashion, the event described in Revelation 20 unveils an even greater truth, that the kingdom of the devil was never a match for the kingdom of God. Oh, what a day that will be!

*And they went up on the breadth of the earth, and compassed the camp of the saints about, and the beloved city: and **fire came down from God out of heaven**, and devoured them. (Revelation 20:9)*

The final conflict of all humanity will be won without the Lord Jesus or any in his ranks needing to "lift a sword." They will just stand and watch God win the battle for them—the salvation of God. This type of thing has happened so many times in the Old Testament; what a fitting way for God to end the dimension of time. The fire coming down from God out of heaven is nothing less than the Creator coming to be with those he created, which was his great passion or wrath all along. The glory of the Lord will be revealed for all flesh to see.

> *And I saw a great white throne, and him that sat on it, from whose face the earth and the heaven fled away; and there was found no place for them. (Revelation 20:10)*

This is the day of God. Notice that the earth and heaven flee away from his face. Again, this is how the same event was recorded in 2 Peter:

> *But the day of the Lord will come as a thief in the night; in the which the heavens shall pass away with a great noise, and the elements shall melt with fervent heat, the earth also and the works that are therein shall be burned up. Seeing then that all these things shall be dissolved, what manner of persons ought ye to be in all holy conversation and godliness, Looking for and hasting unto the coming of the day of God, wherein the heavens being on fire shall be dissolved, and the elements shall melt with fervent heat? (2 Peter 3:10–12)*

Conclusion

Let's continue with our new perspective. Are we now looking at the correct picture box wherein all the pieces will fit?

And I saw the dead, small and great, stand before God; and the books were opened: and another book was opened, which is the book of life: and the dead were judged out of those things which were written in the books, according to their works. And the sea gave up the dead which were in it; and death and hell delivered up the dead which were in them: and they were judged every man according to their works. And death and hell were cast into the lake of fire. This is the second death. And whosoever was not found written in the book of life was cast into the lake of fire. (Revelation 20:12–15)

God has returned in all his glory, and the "earth and heaven" fled away. He then sets up His throne where the final judgment will be given to those who did not partake in the judgment of his Son during the first resurrection. Verses 12 through 15 are a summation of God's perfect justice being meted out to them.

Verse 12 speaks of "books" and "another book," which it defines as the "book of life." It goes on to say that the dead would be judged out of the things written in the "books" according to their works. Would it not make sense that these would be the books of the law: Leviticus, Deuteronomy, etc.?

These verses stand as a testament to the perfect fulfillment of all that was written in the Word of God regarding all the dispensations of time. Those believers of the Old Testament who looked forward to the coming of the Messiah were ready to bow immediately before him when in his presence. Those who did not make a decision in their lifetimes received a second chance and will eventually repent and receive the salvation he came to bring.

But those in the final group who would not respond to any of the attempts God made to save them, who refused his love, kindness, mercy, and forgiveness in Christ, will consequently have to base their eternal salvation on their own works instead. And we all know what that means:

> *Now we know that what things soever the law saith, it saith to them who are under the law: that every mouth may be stopped, and all the world may become guilty before God.* ***Therefore by the deeds of the law there shall no flesh be justified in his sight****: for by the law is the knowledge of sin. But now the righteousness of God without the law is manifested, being witnessed by the law and the prophets; Even the **righteousness of God which***

Conclusion

is by faith of Jesus Christ unto all and upon all them that believe: *for there is no difference:*

For all have sinned, and come short of the glory of God; Being justified freely by his grace through the redemption that is in Christ Jesus: Whom God hath set forth to be a propitiation through faith in his blood, to declare his righteousness for the remission of sins that are past, through the forbearance of God; To declare, I say, at this time his righteousness: that he might be just, and the justifier of him which believeth in Jesus. (Romans 3:19–26)

There was only one man who was able to live every jot and tittle of the law perfectly. Without Jesus accomplishing that for us, and God freely giving the justification to righteousness to all who believe, none of us would stand a chance. Yet these individuals of their own freewill were deceived into refusing this grace and mercy, so they must face the Great White Throne based on their own merits and will therefore fail. Along with death and hell, they will be consumed by the cleansing fire of God's presence. What an amazing God! The perfect judge!

And in case there's any question that this final event is not an angry God in his fury, but just a loving God reunited with his children, which has been his passion or "wrath" all along, let's look at the opening verses of chapter 21:

> *And I saw a new heaven and a new earth: for the first heaven and the first earth were passed away; and there was no more sea. And I John saw the holy city, new Jerusalem, coming down from God out of heaven, prepared as a bride adorned for her husband. And I heard a great voice out of heaven saying, Behold,* **the tabernacle of God is with men***, and* **he will dwell with them***, and they shall be his people, and* **God himself shall be with them***, and be their God. (Revelation 21:1-3)*

The truth of God being with humanity is said three times in verse 3, so there's absolutely no way to get it wrong.

> *And I saw no temple therein: for the Lord God Almighty and the Lamb are the temple of it. And the city had no need of the sun, neither of the moon, to shine in it: for the glory of God did lighten it, and the Lamb is the light thereof. (Revelation 21:22-23)*

It's all pretty clear that the heart's desire of the Creator God is once again fulfilled as he gets to dwell among his

Conclusion

people. That's all he ever wanted. Can you just imagine what that's going to be like?

> *And there shall be no more **curse**: but the throne of God and of the Lamb shall be in it; and his servants shall serve him. (Revelation 22:3)*

The three things that were cursed back in Genesis chapters 3 and 4 exist no longer: the earth, the devil, and his seed. Some of the translations of "there shall be no more curse" render it "nothing that God judges guilty." How about the Amplified Bible, Classic Edition:

> *There shall no longer exist there anything that is accursed (detestable, foul, offensive, impure, hateful, or horrible). But the throne of God and of the Lamb shall be in it, and His servants shall worship Him [pay divine honors to Him and do Him holy service]. (Revelation 22:3)*

Oh, by the way, remember Moses' request of God on Mount Sinai? He had a relationship with God unlike any other, "face to face, as a man speaketh unto his friend." Yet he could not see God in his glory at that time; his request was denied, and he was told just a few verses later:

*And he said, Thou canst not see my **face**: for there shall no man see me, and live. (Exodus 33:20)*

With darkness and all accursed things having been purged, the request of Moses from thousands of years ago is now granted and extended to all:

And they shall see his face. (Revelation 22:4)

---
*The Companion Bible, page 1161.

www.ingramcontent.com/pod-product-compliance
Lightning Source LLC
Chambersburg PA
CBHW022103090426
42743CB00008B/694